Inspiring | Educating | Creating | Entertaining

Brimming with creative inspiration, how-to projects, and useful information to enrich your everyday life, Quarto Knows is a favorite destination for those pursuing their interests and passions. Visit our site and dig deeper with our books into your area of interest: Quarto Creates, Quarto Cooks, Quarto Homes, Quarto Lives, Quarto Drives, Quarto Explores, Quarto Gifts, or Quarto Kids.

© 2015 Quarto Publishing Group USA Inc.
Text © 2015 Maria Colletti
Photography © 2015 Maria Colletti unless otherwise noted below

First Published in 2015 by Cool Springs Press, an imprint of The Quarto Group,
100 Cummings Center, Suite 265-D, Beverly, MA 01915, USA.
T (978) 282-9590 F (978) 283-2742 QuartoKnows.com

Cool Springs Press titles are also available at discount for retail, wholesale, promotional, and bulk purchase. For details, contact the Special Sales Manager by email at specialsales@quarto.com or by mail at The Quarto Group, Attn: Special Sales Manager, 100 Cummings Center, Suite 265-D, Beverly, MA 01915, USA.

ISBN: 978-1-59186-633-6

Library of Congress Cataloging-in-Publication Data

Colletti, Maria, 1959- author.
  Terrariums : gardens under glass : designing, creating, and planting modern indoor gardens / Maria Colletti.
     pages cm
  Includes index.
  ISBN 978-1-59186-633-6 (sc)
1. Glass gardens. 2. Terrariums. 3. Indoor gardening. I. Title. II. Title: Gardens under glass.

SB417.C65 2015
635.9'824--dc23

2015012059

Acquisitions Editor: Billie Brownell
Project Manager: Caitlin Fultz
Art Director: Cindy Samargia Laun
Book Design and Layout: Amelia LeBarron

Photo Credits
Lori Adams: front cover, 1, 4, 6, 8, 14, 30, 32–34, 36–39, 42, 44, 46 (top), 48, 50, 52, 56–59, 60 (top), 64–66, 68, 74–103, 104 (top right, bottom right), 105–108, 111 (top), 112, 119 (bottom right), 120 (above, top, middle, right), 124 (right), 126 (top right), 129 (top), 132–135, 137, 140, 143 (left), 144, 147–148, 150, 156, 157 (bottom), 158, 160
Daniel L. Hyman: 10, 176
All other photos by Maria Colletti.

TERRARIUMS
GARDENS UNDER GLASS

DESIGNING, CREATING, AND PLANTING
MODERN INDOOR GARDENS

MARIA COLLETTI

COOL SPRINGS PRESS
Home and Garden Experts™

MINNEAPOLIS, MINNESOTA

CONTENTS

INSPIRATION
COMES IN MANY FORMS

Just what *is* a terrarium? Terrariums create an enclosed ecosystem that mimics the natural world. Moisture evaporates from the soil level and the leaves of plants, then condenses on the roof and walls of a glass vessel or container. The condensed vapor then drops down, replicating the natural rain cycles that provide moisture for our ecosystem and keep our planet alive.

In 1829, Dr. Nathaniel B. Ward (1791–1868), a London physician with a passion for botany and nature, realized the scientific principle behind what is now our modern-day terrarium. In a closed bottle, Dr. Ward studied a sphinx moth in its chrysalis and found a fern seedling growing. After four months' time, without so much as a drop of water from him, the seedling developed. Ward was amazed, and the concept for the Wardian case was born. Ward could not have known how he would influence the future of terrarium craft over a century later, but we appreciate his discovery today.

This modern-day Wardian case design is gloriously filled with palms, which are traditional conservatory plants.

Charles Darwin sailed on the ship HMS *Beagle* around the world from 1832 to 1836, including a trip to the Galapagos Islands off South America. In 1839, he published findings that led to his "survival of the fittest" theory. This theory can be boiled down to this: living things pass along the traits (or genes) that best assist in the optimal survival of their species.

Darwin and others brought back botanicals that were kept alive because the explorers transported their finds from the jungles of far-away continents and back to civilization in large glass jars. They had to keep these plant specimens alive to study, draw, and catalog. They chose Dr. Ward's method of enclosed glass jars, which was actually perfect for exotic plant material that naturally lives in hot, humid environments.

On my windowsill at home, I have started my own experiments. I have contained a Venus flytrap or a little creeping fig in a lidded jar. I wake up every morning and peer into its small world to check on its survival. I may open the lid and wipe out the excess moisture, and then close the lid. This amuses me, and I think of myself as a naturalist who has brought home her exotic treasures to grow and study under glass.

I have experimented with carnivorous plants, ferns, and tropical foliage plants, and have also incorporated stones and moss. Now I have successful outcomes, small worlds of all kinds, to share with you. Successful lidded terrariums do not need watering or much maintenance, so you can enjoy them even more.

Do you think Dr. Ward would be proud of how we have developed such loveliness from his scientific beginnings?

The Roots of My Terrarium Obsession

It all started years ago in a place called The Shop in the Garden at The New York Botanical Garden, where I work. At the time, we were selling unusual, uniquely shaped home décor glass vessels. One duplicated an enormous 3-foot-tall martini glass, complete with long stem. I started filling these "glasses" with plants, and they sold!

Terrariums were not as popular or well known then. I kept experimenting, using loads of different plants and scenarios until I found my own design method. I learned which plants I could maintain well, and where the terrarium craft was headed. This was before the air plant mania (*Tillandsia*) rose to its present crescendo. Since that first design, I have created dozens of small-world landscapes encased in glass. It excites me to think my creations are bringing joy to others and exist out there as a small slice of botanical life.

I am a retailer first, but my perspective is that of a garden lifestyle retailer. My perspective is unique in that I am always thinking: where can I get these plants, this material, or these supplies? Do I have to have it shipped it to me, or can I find it conveniently in my neighborhood?

So in addition to sharing my terrarium design and growing experience, I am passing the results of my resource searches to you, the terrarium lover, the terrarium designer, or the new terrarium hobbyist who says, "I want to try out a new craft. I want a living thing near me where I can see it every day. Maybe I need it to take up very little amount of my free time and space."

This Venus fly trap (*Dionaea* species) lived in this jar for several years with no bugs to eat yet still survived and *grew*.

MARIA'S INSIDER TIPS

What I share in this book I have learned firsthand from doing things myself. I am sharing with you years of experience about what worked for me and what did not. So my advice is the result of terrariums that I have actually designed, created, and maintained, not from research.

I'll also be sharing tips from other industry retailers, growers, and terrarium designers who are happy to share their expertise with you as well. So this book will be a resource for everyone from a novice amateur to a budding expert professional.

My inspiration on this day during the summer of 2013 was the colorful garden of flowering annuals at the Golden Gate Park sitting in front of the Conservatory of Flowers, located in San Francisco, California. I just cannot resist a chance to sit among the flowers.

Does this sound appealing to you? Let this book be your indispensable guide on your trip to terrarium nirvana! You will find pages full of mail-order suppliers in the Resource Guide, as well as a listing of regional retailers and plant nurseries that are creating extraordinary terrarium displays and holding workshops. I have discovered living-moss growers who are scrambling to keep up with the demand this new pastime has brought to our lives. And because I support local businesses whenever possible, I've included many that I've found close to me. But check out *your* area; there may be terrarium craftspeople selling at florists, church bazaars, or farm stands near you—buy local when you can!

Our electronic devices are pulling us further away from the natural world. But why not use Twitter, Pinterest, Instagram, and Facebook to connect you to even more terrarium ideas long after you have consumed this book's instructions. Wherever you happen to live, whether it's Brazil, Jakarta, the UK, or the United States—everyone is passionate about their creations. Connect yourself to all of the collective artistry in our creative world.

What's Next?

Where is all this leading you? Think of yourself as a garden designer on a minuscule scale. You are not just plunking a few plants into a glass jar; you're actually *designing* a garden or recreating a landscape from nature. Think of your favorite places or the gardens that you love in the world. Where is your favorite outdoor spot? What is your favorite garden design? Take elements

SHOPPING FOR INSPIRATION

There are many resources to be found at your area shopping malls too. Many popular home décor shops such as Anthropologie, West Elm, Pottery Barn, Crate & Barrel, IKEA, and even retailers like Target are incorporating terrarium materials that can be purchased alongside kitchen equipment, floor rugs, or apparel. I often browse the sales floors of these stores for ideas on how to display terrariums in my home or office. Their visual merchandisers must come up with clever in-store displays to entice shoppers to bring home some item they *must* have. I confess that I get pulled right in and often buy something to add to my own terrarium kits or for my next instructor workshop experience or own home collection.

Retailers are stocking all kinds of glass containers just waiting for us to fill them with gravel and plants. Anchor Hocking, a company that has been supplying glass cookie jars and storage containers to the food industry for years, is now marketing some of its inventory as homes for terrariums. Everyone is getting in the act.

from these ideas and places, and reduce them into their essential components to transform them into gardens under glass.

Terrariums are a wonderful way to return to the beautiful world we see around us in our parks, gardens, historic estates, seashores, forests, and deserts—but to do it indoors, as we crave the natural world in our homes and workspaces. There is such a sweet pride in creating and sustaining a small garden that you can peer into every day. I promise you will marvel at your abilities.

I hope that you find plenty of inspiration on these pages to fill endless numbers of glass containers with your terrarium designs. I find it's the small things in life that bring us great joy. It is my pleasure to bring a little joy into your life—one terrarium at a time.

Let's get started right now. Remember—be inspired and *create*!

Maria

GARDEN INSPIRATION

Be inspired! This is what I say to myself—and this is what I say to you.

You never know what will impress you or where you will find inspiration. I created a large Victorian terrarium design inspired by the Abby Aldrich Rockefeller garden in Seal Harbor, Maine. I built this terrarium during an exhibit commemorating the private garden, which was featured at The New York Botanical Garden in the Enid A. Haupt Conservatory during the summer of 2014.

Mrs. Rockefeller's garden is Asian-inspired and designed by landscape architect Beatrix Farrand (1872–1959), who was the niece of writer Edith Wharton. It contains a moss-covered stone path to a moon gate lined by tall, majestic ferns.

In this vintage Wardian case, I wanted to display aspects of that celebrated Maine garden. I decided to employ a trick and used a backdrop representing the moon gate. You can view the tiny *Podocarpus nerifolius* through the opening.

Be inspired by such gardens, or by your own backyard!

ABOVE: This photo shows a lovely *Podocarpus* close-up viewpoint of the interior of this terrarium.

LEFT: The photo shows the terrarium replica where I used a hard resin steppingstone path, obtained from a fairy garden supplies vendor, to mimic a real path and buried it in dried sheet moss. It works very well to recreate the scene.

CHAPTER 1

TERRARIUM DESIGN

In this chapter, I share my favorite terrarium designs. These designs mimic the natural world, such as a woodland, desert, bog, or tropical jungle. In these concept designs, I will add fundamentals of small garden design, maybe a bench, a stream, a dry riverbed, or a gravel pathway.

Even the simplest glass container is elevated to a splendid garden by the details we meticulously place inside. I will highlight how we create variation by using these details in similar containers. Sometimes, I will use one exceptional plant because it is so attractive, even if it has to be a temporary glass house resident. The detail was worth its moment in time!

The use of one distinctive plant can influence your design and change the "feel" or "style" of your terrarium. You'll see how distinctive plants influence each of the terrarium design in this chapter:

- Tropical Terrariums
- Variations on a Fish Bowl
- Woodland Flavor
- Desert Landscapes
- Seasonal Terrariums

In glass garden design, we use basic ingredients to change the miniature landscape and create a unique place taken from our memories of the beauty in the real world we admire.

HOW TO TRANSLATE NATURE INTO TERRARIUM DESIGNS

Even though my terrarium gardens are an extension of my love of the natural world, I also love designed outdoor gardens. Garden design encompasses so many ideas and concepts that we can try to incorporate into terrariums.

For example, there are formal, gravel, perennial, or seaside gardens. There are gardens that reflect historical importance or create mystery, such as a secret garden. There are gardens that include influences from around the world, such as English, French, or Italian gardens. Gardens in the United States often reflect one region of our country, such as the Northwest climate in Seattle, or the hot, steamy gardens of the South. There are the four distinct seasons in Pennsylvania at Longwood Gardens of Kennett Square, one of my favorite places to visit.

Each of these styles includes decorative elements that are unique to them. Maybe it's a bridge placed over a man-made stream, or a hedge, or a sundial placed in the center of an herb garden, or a winding brick path to a sitting area with a bench.

I offer these garden design concepts to further stimulate your imagination. Think about what you might include in your design.

Plants' Influence on Design

Consider tropical plants and their many differences. Consider their height, leaf textures, variegation, and growth patterns. Are they upright or prostrate? Maybe they are vines that creep around the moss or groundcovers that spread outward? Are the colors of their leaves red, chartreuse, white-striped, or mottled?

What plant choices would be best for your preferred garden design style? The regional climate you want to emulate? What natural landscape do you want to create? Take the idea further: incorporate one garden element in miniature or recreate an authentic replica of places you've visited as you traveled around the world.

TERRARIUM DESIGNS

Let's look at some finished terrariums. Read the triangle design theory in Chapter 4 on page 74. Look closely at each full terrarium garden and trace the plants in their step down pattern. Each design is planted closely, with leaf textures and colors contributing to the overall finale. Your eye should move from tall to small, darker to lighter, throughout the design.

Tropical Terrariums

Tropical Palm Glass Triangle ▶

This glass jar is triangular, with a well-fitting gasket around the lid. There are three types of moss covering the soil with a layer of pea gravel in the drainage area that shows nicely through the glass bottom. The living moss on the left is a *Selaginella apoda*; in the center is dried chartreuse reindeer moss; and in the right corner is dried sheet moss. The trio of plants includes arrowhead (*Syngonium podophyllum*), *Fittonia* (my favorite), and an airy fern, *Pteris*. This fern has oddly shaped rectangular leaflets on long stems that wave in the air. The copper garden element is a bird feeder; it waits for an imaginary songbird to perch upon it.

This terrarium will live contently without being opened for months. No maintenance will be required except maybe pulling out a dead leaf or two once a year—I swear!

Tropical Foliage Jar ▶

This is traditional lidded jar. It uses common pea gravel in the drainage area as well as in the topdressing. The plant in the forefront is a dark-leaved *Peperomia* 'Schumi Red'. *Peperomia* are sturdy plants that hold up well. An autumn fern is fanning out above. I felt that the small copper watering can was a cute addition.

This terrarium will last quite a long period of time, maybe a year, and not need any care because this lidded style of glass container holds moisture very well. Please note: the photo of this design was taken outside in plenty of sunlight, but you should *never* allow a terrarium to sit outside or in this much sunlight because, as you see, it is sweating profusely and will eventually bake in the heat.

◄   Open Glass Trio

I adore *Tillandsia tectorum*, or air plant, sitting among other foliage like a sea urchin or spidery insect. Here, it sits on dried sheet moss (*Hypnum*) and there are a few larger, smooth white stones in view under the *Philodendron*. The open terrarium, a palm-sized open glass holder that is curved at the top, is sitting on a blue ceramic plate that says, "Notice me!"

This perfect group of plants has three very different looks that complement one another well. The air plant looks great with coral-colored *Philodendron* and a cascading variegated English ivy (*Hedera helix*) spilling over the front edge. In terms of maintenance, the air plant can be plucked out for watering, the ivy should be pinched back regularly to strengthen its stems, and the *Philodendron* will grow taller (either replace it eventually or prune it).

Half Moon #1   ▶

This upright, half-moon vessel appeared in Martha Stewart's online shop a few years ago. At the time, I was experimenting with unconventional glass containers and how the usual plant suspects would play out when used for their growth patterns alone. The design I created has a healthy piece of dried *Dicranum* mood moss in the center while the *Neanthe bella* palm slides up the rear glass wall at its peak. A *Pteris* fern on the left circles around to cover the soil. The final design was appealing and a successful experiment.

HALF MOON MAINTENANCE

These upright half-moon glass containers are easy to care for, like most terrariums. That is part of their popularity, low to no maintenance. The soil base is small, maybe an inch thick, so shoot two to three strong streams of water into each plant's base to wet the rootball at least once a week.

◀ Half Moon #2

This half-moon vessel is full of dried chartreuse reindeer moss (*Cladina*) with three plants pulled together like a tropical bouquet. Arrowhead (*Syngonium podophyllum*) sits at the top of the triangular design with bird's nest fern (*Asplenium nidus*) hiding its stems, while leatherleaf fern (*Rumohra adiantiformis*) is hugging it below and hanging over the outer edge. This style can fit on a bookcase, shelf, or desk as a green spot of garden life always in view.

◀ Half Moon #3

For the rear of this design, I placed a striking arrowhead with white center vein. In the center is a *Pteris* fern again, but I've slipped an angel wing begonia (*Begonia coccinea*) in front. I've also placed a bit of leaf-green reindeer moss on the right and sheet moss on the left to topdress the soil.

Square Large #1 ▶

I created this large, open, square, glass container for a Spruce Home & Garden store (previously located in Bronxville, New York), for a coffee table setting. (I think terrariums in retail settings make a store so inviting, whether you purchase one or just admire them as you pass by them.) In order to keep the weight down, I planted halfway up with a selection of groundcover plants to glance into from above.

The plant on the left is Irish moss (*Sagina subulata*), a groundcover that has the most interesting fuzzy structure; it makes a design look lush. The center *Hypoestes* plant in red pulls your eye down, and the love of my life, baby tears

(*Helxine soleirolii*) begins to move into creeping fig (*Ficus pumila*). In the right-hand corner there is sheet moss, and in the left corner there is gravel. The plants are the stars, so the topdressing is minimal; clean lines accent a home décor display.

◀ Square Large #2

The same square container is used here, but with a fuller selection. The green gravel shows nicely in the design. The tallest rear plant is a *Dracaena* set right up against the back corner with *Peperomia* flanking its right and bird's nest fern (*Asplenium nidus*) on the left. A dry gravel stream divides the strawberry begonia (*Saxifraga stolonifera*) from a button fern (*Pellaea rotundifolia*) at the right corner, up against the glass.

I like this full jungle of plants. It is easy to care for because none of these plants require much fuss. They hold water well, and there is a large soil base to keep their roots moist. Here, I left the soil exposed. I think the jungle speaks for itself.

Variations on a Fish Bowl

Here we consider the humble fish bowl with a variety of interior gardens. Even when the shape is repeated, the imagination is unlimited.

Cryptanthus #1 ▶

This is my favorite custom-made design. My customer picked out the plants and said to me, "I'll be back in an hour; impress me." The basis for this design is two very strong focal points that overlap and flow together for visual effect.

The color scheme is a pinkish fuchsia-mauve variation so the chartreuse lime green of the Spanish moss combines softly. It is a gentle color scheme. The

textural changes of each plant make for an eye-catching design. I admit that for a short period, I was obsessed with *Cryptanthus*; here's how I did it.

I used a rich green, flat sheet of preserved moss to lay a soft bed for the *Cryptanthus* 'Pink Star' to sit upon. The mixture of river stones in gray, white, black, and browns add another dimension on the opposite side; they move your eye downward from the 'Pink Star'. The river stones were purposely placed underneath the radiating leaves of the *Cryptanthus*. I moved the stones around so they would deliberately amassed on one side of the container.

The air plant (*Tillandsia*) is delicately placed in the spot where it overlaps onto the 'Pink Star'. The air plant sits high in the design, allowing the tips to peak out of the rim of the container. It can easily be pulled in and out for proper soaking each week and definitely has the air circulation it needs. Right in the middle is a small *Alternanthera*. This is a thin-leaved variety with a blue-green hue that fits nicely with the greenish stripe down the middle of the *Cryptanthus* and the air plant.

Notice all three plants have a growth style that radiates outward to a pointed tip. This creates a cohesive visual effect in the overall design.

Crypthanthus #2 ▶

This is the inside view of a giant brandy glass terrarium. I wanted the glass vessel to fit the overall theme of something vintage yet distinguished because the finished terrarium was to be auctioned off at an antique show near my hometown.

In this rendition, the *Cryptanthus* is slightly to the side on a bed of dried preserved green sheet moss. The reason that I chose to use the solid green sheet moss was to give the *Cryptanthus* 'Pink Star' a platform to showcase its striking drama. The accompanying plants are *Fittonia* and *Ficus pumila repens*. Both the smaller plants nestled together have white accents. The white pops out and pulls your eyes to them both. The pebble bits are a neutral color so

they do not compete with the rest of the plants. In this overall design, I used plants with smooth textured leaves so their white veins and leaf outlines act as the textural variances. I feel it is effective.

◄ *Cryptanthus* #3

Sometimes I just want the green world around me in a glass container close at home, so that is the predominant color scheme here. I wanted to see lush verdant moss, petite ferns, and age-old *Selaginella*. The fern on the left is a lighter green button fern (*Pellaea rotundifolia*) that will grow a bit larger to fill out the space and offset the center focal plant, *Cryptanthus*. The *Selaginella* moss on the right competes for space around the edges; it can be snipped and pruned if needed. But watching it grow and move over the preserved mound of *Dicranum* moss between them on the left will be an appealing lesson in natural cause.

Where a terrarium is displayed is important, because where the surroundings will enhance its contents. The surface will reflect off the glass and add to the color of the interior design. To take this photo, I placed this luxuriant emerald world on a green ceramic birdbath because it suited its fertile sophistication.

Cryptanthus #4 ►

Here you see how a fern can arch over the *Cryptanthus* 'Pink Star' and produce a feathery aspect to the scene. *Fittonia* is buried a bit more into the moss and smothered ever so slightly with the *Selaginella* on purpose. Again, using mostly green with lots of moss and the fern creates a more woodsy effect; the only other color is the 'Pink Star', which makes it even more striking.

Cryptanthus #5 ▶

I find this selection attractive and eye-catching because the red-vein *Fittonia* is the real celebrity instead of the 'Pink Star'. The *Fittonia* will also grow to tower over the rest of the specimens, which I think will change the design in an interesting way. By using larger black stones, the tone of the arrangement has an increased intensity while the bowl contains a green swirl in the glass itself. This variety of *Selaginella* 'Ruby Red' I used is amazing with its dark branching.

Mounded dried mood moss will hold its shape while the plants curve over it, and it doesn't need water. You can think of it as a display prop to showcase the other three plants.

Woodland Flavor

Woodland Flavor #1 ▶

This fish bowl has a pop of white reaching up to you. I used *Hypoestes*, commonly called polka dot plant, in its white form. It is the tallest plant in the circle and has several plants in its understory, just like a woodland park. Small and sweet autumn fern (*Dryopteris erythrosora*) is placed center, but deep. The strawberry begonia (*Saxifraga stolonifera*) adds visual texture with fuzzy growth on its leaf pads and by the way those pads hover above the moss. It pulls the white and green colors together. *Selaginella kraussiana* is used again, but it's a different variety.

I added river stones in a snaking pattern through the center, from one side to the other, in an effort to mimic a dry creek bed. It reminds me of hiking days on the Appalachian Trail and how wonderful I feel in the forest.

Woodland Flavor #2 ▶

This design creates the sense of an engaging woodsy forest, like you might come across on a hike. The center *Selaginella erythropus*, with its darker form and higher branching, resembles a woodland plant surrounded by autumn fern (*Dryopteris erythrosora*) to the left. A slight hue of pink on the arrowhead (*Syngonium podophyllum*) matches the center plant's coloring. Arrowhead does grow taller, but in a tightly planted container, that process will slow down. Prune out any taller leaves as they pop up over the lid. A tiny cutting of creeping fig (*Ficus pumila*), all green in color, will grow a bit more to circle the outside of the terrarium or it can be contained by trimming.

These four plants work softly together to give the terrarium an earthy feel. I added some smaller black pebbles to accent and break up the moss. I just like how you feel when you look at this design. It creates a pleasant emotion, giving you that sense of a deep breath.

Desert Landscapes

Dry terrariums are some of the most playful designs. You can change up the colors of the sand, create soft succulent scenes, or plant dramatic cactus with dagger-like needles. My designs ideas were formulated out of places where I

WATER BEFORE PLANTING

Remember to water your plants *before* planting by dipping their roots in a water bath. You do not want to pour water on your new desert landscape. You will bury the succulents or cactus with their soil-covered, watered rootballs intact so when the dry landscape needs moisture (many weeks after planting time), the soil will hold the water and the plant's roots can drink.

have traveled. My thoughts returned to Tucson, Arizona, and its saguaro cacti. Saguaros are tall, majestic, and wave at one another over scrubby tumbleweeds in a sandy terrain.

Sometimes you will see a breathtaking place while browsing through a magazine from your living room chair and be inspired to recreate a small part of it. Your dry garden can mimic the Mexican Sonoran Desert or the Baja coastline.

Two Half-Moon Sisters ▶

These twin, open, half-moon glass dishes sit together like two cousins, and they were effortless to complete. You essentially pour some sand in the base, pull the small plants out of their 2-inch pots, set them in the vessel, and pour more sand over their rootballs until they're completely buried. As you see, I tossed some conch shells into the mix, but authentically this design does not resemble a beach; it's more a desert scene. The pebbles are pearl stones, which catch the light and shimmer slightly.

The plants in the glass dish on the right are jade plants (*Crassula*), with a single stem needleless cactus among a winding row of pearl rocks. In the glass dish on the left, there are two *Echeveria* and three small aloe seedlings. *Escheveria* grow slowly and require no maintenance except a squirt of water now and then from your mister. I added two larger, white, smooth stones but I buried them a bit like you would see in nature.

White Stones & Green Succulents ▶

A succulent collection in a large open container looks great with a tumble of larger stones tossed in the forefront. The center plant is a jade plant, and an *Escheveria* is located behind a mini *Haworthia* on the right. Another idea: you could create a outer circle of pebbles at the bottom of the glass container and

pour soil in the center. If you can hide the soil at the glass wall, then the colors remain white, natural and more desert-like—which is more authentic. I prefer my landscape designs to be truer to the natural environment they are representing.

◄ Opuntia in Sand

The purity of the sand coverage and the soft natural colors of an *Opuntia* cactus poking out the top is a great look. The sand holds well above the larger gravel (although I did put a paper divider between the layers to prevent the sand from sifting through to the bottom). The cactus is poking its ears out of the sand with *Lithops* and a tiny *Aloe* to keep it company. I placed flat, smooth, white stones and threw in a few shells for texture. The sand was provided from a cactus vendor, so it is clean and the proper material for this planting.

Wonderful *Opuntia* cactus has many varieties, and this one is close to the pomegranate variety, maybe the species *dillenii*. *Opuntia microdasys*, commonly called bunny ears, has fuzzy bunches on its pads that are actually needles. They stick in your skin and itch, so don't touch!

◄ African Lithops Dry Landscape

This is one of my favorite succulent desert designs with luscious-looking living stones hiding among the natural stones with a perfectly pale *Echeveria rosette*. I used brown-colored slate chips the same color as the *Lithops* to copy the African terrain where they live camouflaged among stones and sand. In this arrangement, I used a very soft builder's sand that has bits and pieces of tiny gravel throughout. This rendition has a genuinely natural landscape look, complete with a dry riverbed across the center. I placed a petrified dragonfly inside to give viewers the idea that things die in the desert without water. I am instantly transported to the deserts of the world and nature's cycle of life. You can replicate this in your terrarium.

Seasonal Terrariums

Seasonal displays can be created with clever nods to hearts for St. Valentine's Day, Easter egg hunts, Fourth of July flags flying, or December holiday folly.

I have shared many of my terrarium combinations in this chapter. It has taken me years to find my personal style. Yes, sometimes I often use similar plants that seem common in the marketplace or fish bowls that are widely available in pet shops. But I always try a new mix of decorative ingredients and planting mediums to create a fresh style. I mix and match the same plants to create something brand new.

The smallest poinsettia (*Euphorbia pulcherrima*) is buried under an avalanche of white sand next to an asparagus fern (*Asparagus densiflorus*), and a Norfolk Island pine (*Araucaria heterophylla*) standing in for a pine tree. These three plants will last a few months in sand, so add a small drainage well at the bottom, maybe incorporating a color of gravel that will enhance your holiday color scheme, such as green, white, or red.

SNOW SCENE TRICK

Use this simple building trick when creating a snow scene. First, lay out a perimeter of white sand and leave an empty interior space. Place the plants in the empty space and bury them in a bit of soil to hold moisture for their roots. This soil will be hidden from view in the next step. Then you use a screen either of black landscape cloth or nylon stocking cut to fit. Lay the fabric over the soil almost to the glass walls, then, using a funnel, pour in the white sand until it completely covers all the dark soil.

I usually find myself surprised at the final product. I often think, "Oh, that looks sweet!" This comes from a genuine inner freedom where I promise to try what may seem odd or unusual and fiddle and move around my building components until a satisfaction sets in and know I like how it looks.

Designing terrariums requires an individual perspective. You will find your personal style. Each person has preferred materials, landscapes, regions, or garden designs that they naturally gravitate toward. Let your preferences guide you toward a terrarium design that you will love—and be inspired to create something new!

SNOW SCENE BUILDING STEPS

I pull out plastic tubs of white sand when the holidays arrive. In December, I use this basic ingredient to mimic pristine, pure white snow, combining it with brown pinecones and faux red berries to create hanging snow globes in glass orbs.

There are several tricks to building this type of terrarium display. First, decide if this is going to be a temporary terrarium. If so, you do not need to fuss with charcoal or drainage material because you will only need it survive for the holidays, maybe four to six weeks.

The next step involves creating the "snow cover." You must use a funnel with this step because sand flies. Place your funnel directly at soil level, exactly where you want the sand to fall. Continue placing the funnel and then pouring sand until you have complete coverage and no longer see any soil. Smooth out the sand with a gentle tap or shake of the glass container.

If there are gaps, think about covering them with more sand or pinecones, plastic deer, or even a holiday tree ornament. I have added small cardboard-house tree ornaments that make it look like there was a village of trolls living in my terrarium. If the ornaments are too big to fit the space, you can remove the faux snow-covered thatch roofs and place just the roof right in between the plants. I particularly like this small snow-covered village look.

Think of how the Grinch looked down from his mountaintop, peering at Cindy Lou Who's village in *How the Grinch Stole Christmas*. Use this vision to inspire your own Dr. Seuss-ian terrarium.

Good sources of garden elements often come from the ornaments sold at holiday time. Gather small bunny or fox ornaments and repurpose them for springtime scenarios.

HANGING SNOW GLOBES WITH AIR PLANTS

Here are a few how-to tips on creating hanging snow globes with air plants and decorations.

1. Sand has a light texture and flies about easily. As you pour, come very close to the globe opening and use a funnel made of paper or plastic, if possible. I actually use a tablespoon quite often, if the opening is large enough.
2. Decide beforehand if your decorative elements will sit to the left or right before placing them. Gingerly place some small stones, miniature pinecones, plastic mistletoe with berries, or faux snow-covered pine needles inside the glass globe.
3. The air plant should go in last. Dunk it in a water bath and completely air-dry it before placing the specimen in its new home.

4. Your air plant will require a water mist twice per week. Set your mister on a stream setting and shoot several quick bursts at the air plant only. The sand will moisten a bit but it will also dry. You can, then, smooth it out, if needed.

5. Enjoy your lovely new snow globe during the holiday season as it hangs in a window or on your tree. In the new year, you can swap out these decorations for Valentine's Day or the spring season. Cheers!

◄ This cheerful holiday air plant glass globe can sit on a kitchen windowsill all through December. The message is a reminder to save time for a little joy.

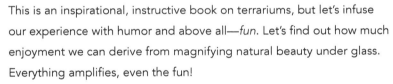

CHAPTER 2

THE BASICS

This is an inspirational, instructive book on terrariums, but let's infuse our experience with humor and above all—*fun*. Let's find out how much enjoyment we can derive from magnifying natural beauty under glass. Everything amplifies, even the fun!

Whether you imagine an exquisite, complex landscape or playful whimsical garden, you'll create those looks with purposely chosen details. In the following sections, you will find plenty of details that will help to create your landscaped theme.

Let's start with the basics for building the foundation of any terrarium. What are "the basics"? These are the ingredients, supplies, tools, and specialty mosses. The basics involve certain sizes and colors of gravel, pebbles, or sand in different colors. All these basic ingredients create a specific look.

You can find these items in traditional terrarium supply websites and at local garden supply stores, among other places. Be sure to rummage through my Resource Guide (page 165) for sources. I find looking for supplies and tools somewhat of a fun-filled scavenger hunt.

TOOLS

I love creating terrarium tools out of household items such as kitchen utensils, but why stop there? Why not make an entire kit of unique terrarium tools that you acquired? Whenever the whim to create hits you, you'll have all the necessary tools at your fingertips.

Specialized Terrarium Tools

You can purchase tools made specifically for terrarium gardening. They are meant to resemble scaled-down garden tools and include a small shovel, a thin digging hoe, and a rake. I think they are wonderful tools, with long handles for reaching into glass vessels, and make great gifts for your special terrarium designer. You can find them on the Internet in stainless steel, metal, or plastic, and yes, they come in handy sometimes. Are they absolutely a necessity? I'll let you be the judge.

Funnels

In terrarium design, I believe in doing things just right. This practice helps create exquisite designs. A funnel is very useful for accurately pouring soil, sand, or water into my terrarium without messing up the design I've created.

Where can you find such funnels? I found the three plastic funnels you see in the photo at auto supply stores, including my red Hopkins super-quick-fill funnel. Most are very inexpensive, usually under five dollars. Get the longest-nosed funnels you can find.

I also make my own paper funnels out of printer paper and tape. You can use any stiff paper that will hold up to the pouring of your basic ingredients, but printer paper is

These teak-handled terrarium tools instantly make you more equipped to care for your terrarium and are stylish looking at the same time.

OPPOSITE: These are indispensable terrarium-building tools: three plastic funnels; a white scoop for pouring soil; a simple fork, knife, and spoon; a chef's basting brush; expert strong tongs; and a soft brush. Make your own terrarium toolkit so that creating terrariums will not only be enjoyable but effortless.

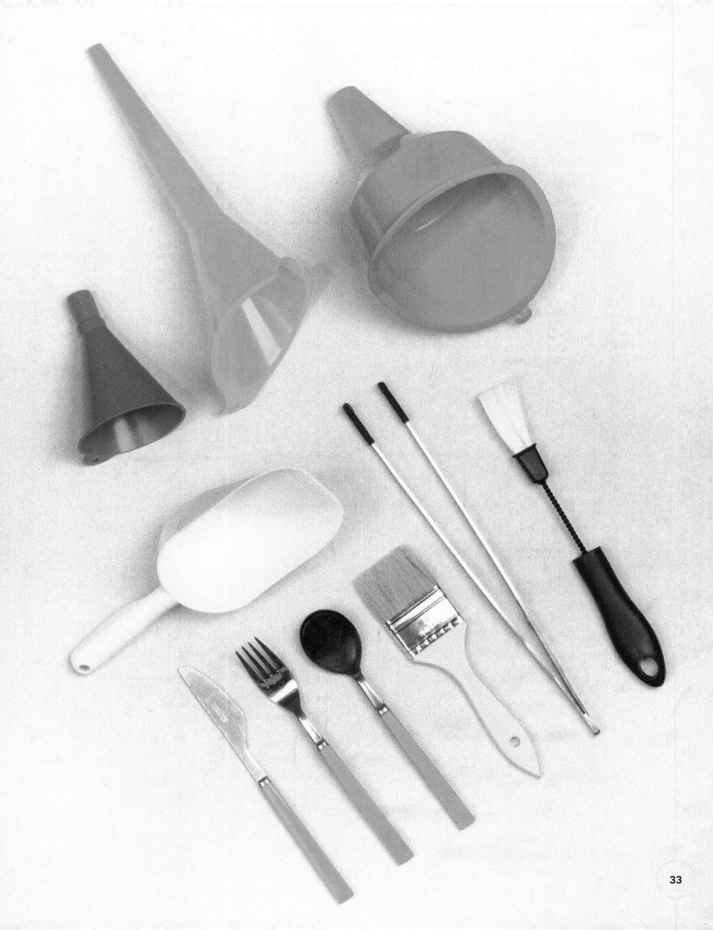

Okay, so why do you need a brush? Many people use brushes to sweep soil off their plants after the design is complete. When you purchase or choose a brush for your terrarium kit, pick one that has very soft, plush bristles. This will protect your plant material from breakage. One idea is to use makeup brushes because they must be quite soft to be used on the skin. Sometimes culinary brushes, which you can find in a restaurant supply store, such as those used to brush butter or sauce onto food, can be useful.

smooth and very flexible: a paper funnel opening can be adjusted to pour soil or pebbles, which is very helpful at the last step when you are adding topdressing. I use them to pour the usual three culprits of mess—soil, sand, or gravel—into my terrarium designs. Neatness makes it possible for each detail of every leaf or moss patch to be seen through the glass.

Brushes

In tropical plant terrariums, I refrain from using brushes because they can break delicate leaves and stems or even displace newly placed plants. Most succulents or cactus can withstand a sweep of a soft bristle brush. Before you begin sweeping the interior of your terrarium, remember to do so with a very delicate, slow touch.

Here is an alternate suggestion for removing debris from your finished design. If you find that soil or some other material has fallen onto your plants and the design has become a bit of a disaster, use a plastic sprayer or mister that has an adjustable tip that can deliver a directed stream of water to wash off the leaves. Do *not* squirt many times because then you would be adding wetness to the problem. Reach into the terrarium as best you can with one hand, and hold the problem leaf or stem between your fingers. Then, with your other hand, shoot a direct squirt onto the leaf—just one, well-aimed shot. This will clean off the messy leaves and help to prevent the extra water from dripping into the soil bed. (See page 156 for more on this technique.)

I admit that I prefer not getting the soil on the leaves in the first place, but that's what's best for me. There is no right or wrong way. Try different strategies and use the one that is most comfortable and successful for your fingers.

Tongs

Tongs are terrific little tools. Chef or restaurant supply stores are great places to hunt for tongs. You can get tongs made of wood, bamboo, metal, aluminum, stainless steel, or just plain plastic. Why use tongs? Tongs help you to pull dead leaves out of your glass jar, move plants and moss around when you're building your design, or just help you reach into tiny spaces that your fingers cannot.

I bought my tongs at a wonderful terrarium supply and design store, Terrain, located in Westport, Connecticut. They are sturdy and made of metal with rubber tips. (They appear in the photo grouping of my toolkit on page 33.) I have seen them offered on Terrain's website (www.terrain.com).

Chopsticks

You should include a pair of chopsticks in your array of helpful utensils. They should be sturdy and not break easily when bent. The wooden chopsticks you get with an Asian meal would be adequate, but you can purchase decorated, fancier chopsticks that are strong and attractive. It is up to you how fashionable your toolkit should be.

You use chopsticks separately—that is, one at a time—to poke and jostle rocks into place or move pieces of preserved moss around and into their proper places. A sturdy stick is just a darn good item to have in your terrarium building kit.

You can purchase these clear plastic scoops from cooking supply stores or other retailers such as The Container Store.

Scoops and Buckets

Having a scoop handy makes planting easier when your hands are full of soil and plant material. I started buying small scoops when I began teaching terrarium workshops. I saw students struggling to pour soil out of the giant plastic bag that I bought from the nursery. So I took the next step and bought a few inexpensive plastic buckets, like a child's sand bucket. I pour a portion of the soil medium into the buckets and place the giant bag of soil or gravel aside. Then students can grab a scoop of soil and easily slide it into their glass containers. Everything stays clean, including hands, so when you handle the plants, they stay clean also. That's the name of the game in terrarium planting—keep everything looking great!

INGREDIENTS

Gravel, Pebbles, and Stones

Gravel, pebbles, and stones have different purposes in designs whether the terrarium containers are open, closed, or unusually shaped designs. These are basic ingredients that can be used as drainage material at the bottom of the terrariums or used instead of potting mix in dry succulent or cactus terrariums or even as final decorative elements.

Gravel comes in many colors that range from black, sandstone, pearl, white, and even the colors of the rainbow. I find gravel to be one of the most important ingredients in terrarium design, besides plants and moss. It represents elements of nature, creates color, and adds layers of visual interest.

It's fun to hunt through aquarium and pet shops for gravel. There are so many colors available, even neon or some that glow in the dark under a black light (if you'd like to try a bit of psychedelia). The aquarium gravel is small

Bowls filled with earthly produce that look good enough to eat.

and works well as topdressing. Using gravel, I have created snake-shaped dry riverbeds in my desert scenes or the Amazon River in my tropical jungles. You can use this method either in a desert scene or through a garden plot to mimic hardscaping in outdoor garden landscapes.

Multi-river stones, which are normally larger than the size of gravel, are also one of my favorite basic ingredients. These small pebbles come in black, white, brown, and natural, with natural cracked lines throughout them.

Sometimes I can get a giant bag of pea gravel from garden supply stores or big home-improvement retailers for less than five dollars. (I drove around with a bag in the trunk of my car for so long that during one winter I threw some of that gravel under my tires to get me out of an icy parking space. Now, *there* is a multipurpose product!) I

BE MINDFUL OF THE ENVIRONMENT

I wash my pea gravel because there is often a great deal of sand in it. I use a plastic strainer or sometimes a metal colander. You *do not* want to do this in your kitchen or bathroom sink because you will be dumping sand down your drain. So either strain pea gravel over your garbage pail or over another pot to catch the unwanted sand, then responsibly dispose of it.

ABOVE: This design uses two colors of sand purchased from the Crayola online shop. Search for colored sand online for many different color choices.

TOP: This demonstrates an exception to using pea gravel. I used larger black stones at the bottom of this thicker glass, I-gallon container so they sit stationary and flat at the bottom of the vessel. You will also see them used in a similar container in a modern indoor water garden on page 147.

love pea gravel because it is the right size of stone to use as drainage material at the bottom of a terrarium. It is inexpensive and easy to find.

Pay attention to the size of the stones you use because if they are larger than gravel or pebbles, they could shift and crack the glass container. Larger stones should only be used as design elements as final touches or in containers with thicker glass walls. Apothecary jars and footed hurricanes can break if the larger stones nestled at the bottom shift under the soil.

Sand

Sand, like our other ingredients, can be used in terrarium designs at the bottom or the top of the soil level, or to bury a succulent's rootball in a dry landscape. Sandtastik and Crayola even offer play sand in colors that range from vivid to more natural.

In certain glass vessels, there may be a footed "well" at the bottom where the sand can fill the space and be fully seen. I cut a paper divider to place on top of this sand layer to keep the soil or gravel layer above from mixing into the sand. Another idea: you can create an old-fashioned layered sand design using various colors. These were popular years ago but have now been brought to a level of modern sophistication.

Glass

Glass chips, crystals, and marbles also are commonly used in terrariums. Combine these elements with feathers, dried flower material, or other natural elements to create a small geological world.

Activated Charcoal

Charcoal is one of those substances that mystifies us by its powers. A solid piece of charcoal that is infused with oxygen,

called activated charcoal, is very porous. It can absorb a large array of odors, molds, and poisons and so purifies the area or material where it is placed, such as in soil or water filters.

Activated charcoal is used in filters in aquariums for the same reason that we use activated charcoal in terrariums. Place shards or pellets of activated charcoal

THE VALUE OF TOPDRESSING

When materials like gravel, sand, or glass are used as topdressing to cover the soil, they prevent moisture from escaping an open terrarium. Much like mulch in the garden, topdressing also finishes off the landscape. It creates neatness and helps the terrarium to actually look like a scaled-down version of our garden world.

More and more national stores are providing topdressing because we, the terrarium customers, have created the demand. I have found many sizes of containers filled with decorative pebbles, glass chips, sand, bark chips, or clear and colored glass marbles. Again, keep your eye out for sources such as Target's floral display section, IKEA's Marketplace (which I find such fun!), Home Goods, Christmas Tree Shops, and of course Michael's or Jo-Ann Fabric and Craft stores. These aren't all the locations you can try; they are just the stores where I've had good luck. Mosser Lee packages a variety of gravel products called "Decorative Soil Cover" or "Decorative Rocks" too.

ACTIVATED CHARCOAL

Here are a few other ways to make use of activated charcoal's absorption powers:

- Use it in a pan in your refrigerator to absorb orders.
- Seal your shoes in a plastic bag with activated charcoal for a few days to eliminate smelly feet odor.
- Place small sachets filled with activated charcoal in closets to remove odors.
- Add a pan of activated charcoal to absorb the moisture in wet basements and eliminate that musty mold smell.

over the drainage material and *under* the soil in the terrarium. It acts as a purifier against mold and fungus.

Potting Soil Mix

The potting soil readily available at retail stores is just fine to use for terrarium planting. Mass producers such as Miracle Gro® blend their potting soil mixtures with perlite (a naturally occurring, white, lightweight volcanic substance) or vermiculite (a beige, granular mineral), to create the drainage. If the potting soil had no such additives, it would turn into a solid mass of wet peat with no air circulation for our plants' root systems. The plants would suffocate, turn black, and eventually die. Remember, water will find a way to drain through the soil to the bottom. Using a potting mix with these additives will prevent a wet mess in the planting area.

Here are some special notes about potting soil:

- African violets thrive in a soil mix of higher acidity, but most plants do not need this specialized potting mix.
- Unless you are planting only cacti or succulents, avoid cactus soil mixture, which contains sand to increase the ability of water to flow through it. Using a cactus potting mix would cause all the water to collect in the drainage well while the soil remained drier than most tropical plants enjoy.
- I tend to be a purist with my designs and want the soil to be absolutely black. I don't like the white bits of perlite showing through the glass. I pick out some of the larger pieces that can be seen at the top or on the sides if I feel they are marring the view.

Bark Chips

Bark chips are a very important ingredient in terrarium building for many reasons. Bark chips change the design with their earthy brown colors and varied shapes. Bark chips can also be used to create the drainage well that is an actual design element at the bottom of the terrarium. You can create multiple layers within a terrarium by alternating bark chips and river stone pebbles. Finally, bark chips make an excellent groundcover around plants, as a topdressing, or as a final design element.

Many retailers sell bark chips, but you can also check out some of the mail-order sites in the Resource Guide (page 165) for more specialized selections. The wholesale company Supermoss 123 markets bags of small, very clean bark chips that are marvelous for this use.

Mosses

This brings us to the most valuable ingredient in our terrarium-building arsenal: moss. Today, event planners use mountains of moss for party décor or table centerpieces. Now, moss is incredibly popular as topdressing, as a dividing layer over drainage components, and as the crucial component of the moss terrarium.

Moss can definitely affect the overall design or style of the terrarium garden you are creating. There are so many choices, so experiment with each type and find your favorites.

Dried and preserved moss is not alive, and it has been treated to retain its appearance. There are many dried and preserved moss products in the marketplace, and there are many types: sheet, reindeer, Spanish, feather, mood moss, and sphagnum.

Sheet Moss

Hypnum curvifolium or *H. imponens* is the botanical name for sheet moss. It has a flat growth pattern, which is why it is called sheet moss. When you flip the moss over, you will find a brown, mat-like, interwoven area (which can be thought of as its root system, but technically, moss has no roots). I have walked through the forests of New York's Catskill Mountains to find sun-dappled paths

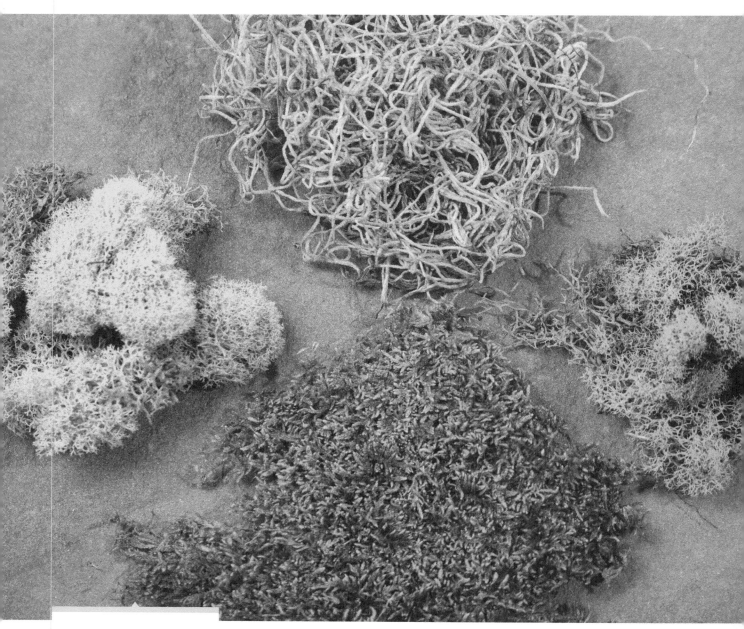

Here are several varieties of moss (starting at top and going clockwise): Spanish moss, chartreuse reindeer moss, sheet moss, and yellow-green reindeer moss. Note the varied textures and colors.

full of sheet moss growing harmoniously on gigantic boulders left there from the long-ago Ice Age.

Its flat nature is what makes this moss so versatile. You can lay it flat over your drainage well between the soil and the activated charcoal. You can create uneven "hills" of soil and cover them with inches of sheet moss to create a green landscape. I mist the dried moss with a bit of water to freshen up the color before placing it in a terrarium.

Sheet moss is often used to make moss balls: a sheet is wrapped around either a Styrofoam ball or a metal frame. I have seen large installation art projects cover beds, cars, and giant topiary forms with moss. So almost anything can be covered by sheet moss.

Living sheet moss can be purchased from moss growers. It holds up well in terrariums and does not normally grow fungus in a well-ventilated glass container. It also makes a good groundcover because it is flat, and you can cut sections from a larger piece to custom fit in your design. You can pull apart living moss, but do *not* break off tiny, ragged pieces: you want to preserve the mat undergrowth as it holds the moss together and takes up moisture and nutrients.

Reindeer Moss

Reindeer moss, or *Cladina*, is not a true moss but a lichen. It looks like a piece of coral, only it is a soft, puffy mass of green. Reindeer moss retains its puffiness in a terrarium, so it can either take up space or be squished into spaces. Lidded or closed terrariums can become too humid, and as the moisture rises, reindeer moss is in danger of becoming moldy. If it does, remove it and replace it with a fresh piece.

This type of "moss" is often seen in different colors: dyed pink, red, chartreuse, coral, blue, purple, dark gray, and white. These varied colors can make for some fantastical looking terrariums. Maybe you'll just want to set some bunches of dark blue reindeer moss in multiple glass globes because the color complements your furniture. Let your creative juices flow!

INSIDER TIPS: MOSS MAGIC

Heidi Masucci is operations manager at Moss Acres in Honesdale, Pennsylvania (www.mossacres.com).

As suppliers to landscapers, how did your company get into the terrarium business?

We found a lot of people asking for smaller orders of moss so they could make terrariums, miniature fairy gardens, and even for placing moss in their dart frog vivariums. We needed to create a smaller package or kit that worked well with ferns in terrariums. So, we created Terrariums & Fairy Garden packs. In these packs, moss will come in a dry, dormant state. This helps keep the moss healthy during shipping. Dampness can create mold and will kill the mosses over time.

Is there any maintenance, practices, or techniques that you would suggest when using mosses in terrariums?

Collected rainwater or distilled water is best to maintain your moss plants. Keeping mosses out of direct sun is best. Never let water bead up on the walls of your terrariums. If this happens, you should open the top until the water evaporates, then close the container again. This should be done as many times as it takes to create dry walls.

Inside this living mood moss terrarium lies the foundation for a miniature Jurassic Park.

Spanish Moss

Spanish moss is an *epiphyte*—that is, a plant that uses another plant as a host for support. Epiphytes, such as mosses, liverworts, lichens, and algae, are found in the temperate zones. Epiphytes in the tropics include orchids, bromeliads, and air plants.

Spanish moss (*Tillandsia usneoides*) looks like gray hair dangling down from the branches of giant oak trees in the southeastern United States. I love movie scenes with mature oak trees lining a long dirt driveway leading to an enormous Southern plantation house. It creates a mood either spooky or dreamy, but always unusual.

Spanish moss, preserved in its natural form or dyed different colors, is easy to tuck in a corner or around a plant, or you can allow it to slide down the narrow neck of a glass bottle. You can drape it from a piece of driftwood, grape wood, or cut branches. It can sit on the bottom of a terrarium vessel or be suspended in a glass globe.

One warning about Spanish moss: in extremely moist, closed terrariums, it tends to rot with fungus. So use it as an accent or replace it often if it gets moldy.

Feather Moss

Feather moss is in the *Ptilium* genus. This type of moss is used less frequently as it is light and does not hold a solid structure. But its loose, feathery structure can be used to create an airy design that will sit loose above the soil. Use a stick to tease this moss into your design.

Mood Moss

I have saved the best for last. I have gone gaga over mood moss and cannot learn enough about it. Mood moss has many common names, but *Dicranum* is its genus. When terrarium building became popular, so did *Dicranum* moss.

Here, I'll discuss the *dried* version of mood moss and how it should be handled. Mood moss grows in a mound-like structure; it appears to be solid, but it can crumble easily. I suggest that you do not pull tiny pieces apart from the whole but instead use mood moss in approximately 2- to 3-inch pieces. Tiny pieces will shred and just won't hold up. But do try using it: find the proper hole or create a special space in your design to fit a mound of mood moss!

Sphagnum Moss

Sphagnum moss is used widely to plant up orchids and Venus flytraps (and other carnivorous plants). Sphagnum moss is the living moss that grows on top of peat bogs, and bogs are a carnivorous plant's favorite place. Decayed, dried sphagnum moss is referred to as *peat moss*, which is a soil conditioner used to enrich dry or sandy landscape soil.

I do not use sphagnum for terrariums because the moss is loose, fiberous, and absorbs and holds a great deal of moisture.

DESIGN ELEMENTS

What is a design element? And why should you use them to decorate your terrarium? A design element can be almost anything, but it definitely is an ingredient that completes your terrarium design. There are two distinct categories: garden elements and found objects.

Here is an example of a garden element: a brown resin garden chair sitting in some club moss (*Selaginella*). It looks like it could be made of twigs, but it is actually plastic.

TOP: Here are examples of toys that can be incorporated into a terrarium. Dinosaurs munching on moss-covered forests seem like a great terrarium design to envision.

BOTTOM: Fabiane Mandarino of Rio de Janeiro, Brazil, has mastered the art of creating an African safari terrarium, like this example, with a giraffe walking among the trees. (Terrariums are called *terrario* in Portuguese.)

The garden element may be a manufactured hard plastic item, such as a tiny animal, or carved from wood, such as a bench or chair. A found object is just that: something found in the outdoors, in our natural surroundings. Of course, found objects can be purchased, such as crystals or rocks.

Design elements bring you into the miniature world. Imagine using flat stones to create stepping stone paths. Lay them inside your terrarium with a bit of space between them. They will lead you to a secret world where you can peer inside for daily reflection.

Garden Elements

A garden element is anything you'd find in an outdoor garden, such as:

- Fountains, birdbaths, statuaries
- Trellises, arbors, pergolas, gates, fences
- Stone pathways, stone walls, stone benches
- Woodland twig benches, trellises

Decorative and fun elements can be many things:

- Plastic replicas of deer, rabbits, frogs, dinosaurs
- Anthropological statues, Roman ruins, bridges

Maybe you found the most lifelike rubber forest toads at a toy store and want to create a woodland fern haven complete with pine trees. (If you do, Norfolk Island pines stand in well for this effect.) You can create an anthropological "dig site" using items found on online. I found an Etsy shop seller who carries Easter Island stone gods. The same site offers cemetery stones for a special Halloween theme. Someone like me who studies anthropology and loves the ruins of the world would love to create a terrarium with a historical theme. Browse Etsy for a theme you might create, and the ideas will begin to flow.

Elements for Fairy Gardens

There is another popular craft rapidly catching momentum: miniature and fairy gardens. Fairy garden suppliers have *plenty* of furniture, garden props, and animals available for sale via mail-order. The Resource Guide on page 165 will lead you to garden benches, birdhouses, birdfeeders, trellises— the list is endless.

I found some terrific vendors and a darling wooden bench at the annual Philadelphia Flower Show (organized by the Pennsylvania Horticultural Society). Check out garden shows or flower shows in your area. You may find similar items at country fairs or city street bazaars right in your neighborhood.

You can also browse what the miniature-house hobby retailers offer for sale and consider model railroad and dollhouse suppliers. Miniature buildings, benches, people, or lifelike stones from these sources can easily be used in terrariums.

Found Objects

A found object is something found in nature: crystals, pinecones, feathers, seashells, nuts, pods, dried

Here is an insect's eye-view inside a terrarium with a copper birdhouse sitting beside a wonderful bead plant (*Nertera granadensis*) full of orange berries.

TREAD LIGHTLY

Please be responsible and cautious if you pick up loose plant material, or a nut or pod that has fallen to the ground, or shells from a beach anywhere on our precious Earth. Remove only the smallest collection of items that you will definitely use and not squander. Our planet thanks you!

Some of the treasures found on adventures of exploration.

flowers, cattails, feathery marsh reeds, branches, grapevines, fallen bird nests, and more.

As a hiker and amateur naturalist, I carry home bits and pieces from my travels. My own scientific exploration has taken me around New York State and beyond. I often pick up items for my still life cloche designs and home décor arrangements such as stems (which also work well in a vase with other stems).

You can do the same for yourself on a walk in your local park or preserve. Take your imagination with you!

CLEAN YOUR FOUND OBJECTS

Remember that anything you collect from nature, especially mosses, may carry insects, fungus, or rotting material back to your home. Clean your found objects, such as shells, stones, or pinecones, to ensure that you have an object free of debris, disease, or pests. Hard objects such as shells, rocks, or stones are easy to wash with soap and water before placing them in your terrarium. It is difficult to clean a piece of moss, but you might want use a stick to dislodge the worms or bugs that have taken up residence. Once I found a small grublike bug sitting on top of my moss in my closed-up jar, so I decided it was time to just put it back outside.

A note on nests: fake bird nests complete with fake eggs are easily sourced at craft stores. If you happen to find an abandoned bird's nest, I do not suggest using it for a few reasons. The birds will return to use it next season, and it will contain muddy soil, insects, and other decaying debris that will not be good for the pristine environment of your terrarium. So please use nests created by crafts suppliers, or perhaps by a local artist, and you will be supporting the craft industry at the same time.

Other natural materials also need special handling. For example, you may want to spray marsh reeds or dried flowers with a substance like hairspray or shellac because they tend to shed willfully. Check out my Still Life Cloche design on page 102 for more information.

Marsh reeds from Pelham Bay Park in Bronx, New York. In the fall in New York, the reeds around marshlands wave with tufts of fluffy, wheatlike tops.

CHAPTER 3

THE GLASS VESSELS

There are *many* styles of glass containers, some with and some without lids. In this chapter, I will cover many terrarium possibilities and help you start your collection of vessels. Even a humble fish bowl can become a masterpiece with your plant and design choices.

Glass vessels include (but are not limited to):

- Fish bowls, footed glass vessels, and cylinders
- Lidded cookie jars and apothecary jars
- Vintage Wardian cases
- Hanging ceramic planters, glass globes, and teardrops
- Cloche displays and lanterns
- Cake stands, compote dishes, and footed fruit bowls

Here, you will learn how to select glass pieces and how they will affect your plant choices. I'll offer my observations on the moisture levels created inside the different container shapes and how you can alter this outcome with a few simple, handy tips. You will learn which containers are good for dry deserts and which are good for humid tropical jungle terrariums.

FISH BOWLS, FOOTED GLASS VESSELS, AND CYLINDERS

These styles are easy to use and easy to find in the marketplace. There are many shapes and styles, and each has its own design considerations. For a design example using a cylinder, see the Soilless Pebble Display project on page 99.

Fish Bowls

The fish bowl is an easy shape to use and one that I especially like. You will find this evident in the many examples in Chapter 1. Fish bowls are often inexpensive and easy to acquire. But that doesn't mean they produce mediocre or visually dull terrariums.

You can easily fit your hands inside the opening of a fish bowl while working the ingredients into the vessel. If you make an incorrect placement, just pull the plant or element out and move it around. Your tools, sometimes just spoons and forks, can dip into the top quickly to move around soil or gravel. Always have your stick at the ready to poke around moss and stones to position them.

Fish bowls sit nicely on home furnishings, such as coffee tables, bookcases, and kitchen counters. You can bring them to your office to make your cubicle space a living green world. Doctors can place them on office reception desks or in waiting rooms. Succulent or air plant arrangements in fish bowls large or small have become favorite table setting décor in restaurants as well as at weddings and events. Wouldn't you *love* to see a gorgeous fish bowl terrarium when you go out to dinner? Of course, the small business owner's retail space can always fit in a terrarium. You get the idea; I think fish bowl terrariums should decorate any space they can fit into.

Why can you put fish bowls in so many areas? Fish bowls can be viewed nearly 360 degrees, from top, sides, or spun around. So when you think about your fish bowl design, decide where it will live for a time and *design it for that space.* If you just want to create in a freeform fashion, then decide where it will fit *best* after it is completed. So many possibilities are available with low, round vessels.

Fish bowls come in many sizes, from miniscule to larger diameters, and extremely large or small bowls require special consideration. I felt daunted when I saw an enormous 18-inch-diameter glass bowl. I wondered how could I fill it with soil and plants and not make it weigh a ton. The key to this size is to plant low in the bowl using only a small amount of planting medium— approximately 1 to 2 inches of depth. Either choose plants that can grow very low and can be viewed looking down on the bowl or choose plants that can tower over the others and fill in the scene. You can let them grow up and out the top. You may have to prune your plants to prevent them from rising without end, but that's okay too. Plants benefit from a snip now and then.

A miniscule fish bowl usually can be found filled with sand, shells, and a small air plant (*Tillandsia*) tucked inside. If you cannot fit your hand inside, you may have to choose plant material that you can just drop in and say "so long" to. You can try moss, not

USING AIR PLANTS IN CYLINDERS

I would not necessarily suggest using air plants (*Tillandsia*) in tall cylinders, where the plant sits low in the container, unless you dry them thoroughly after soaking. Give the air plant a good shake after you take it out of the water bath. Then air-dry these plants on your counter. I like to lay out a paper towel to set them on before returning them to the cylinder. As long as an air plant is given the time to drink in water, and then the water is allowed to evaporate, it will be content to be displayed in a tall cylinder or vase.

sand, and a small plant with a few pebbles on the bottom. Anyway, make it simple and set the tiny world anywhere there is a source of light.

Lidded Fish Bowls

Lidded fish bowls, I have found, create an issue: they sweat condensation. I am not suggesting that you do not use them. They are great, classic, lidded shapes, but you should know that you will have to watch over them a bit. I am no scientist, but I suggest there is something about the circular swoop upward that creates a hot pocket at the roof and increases the amount of water droplets that form on the inside glass walls. If you leave the lid off too long, you risk the chance that your terrarium will dry out more than is necessary and that may possibly wilt the plants beyond recovery. At that point, you may just have to water it. The cycle keeps repeating itself. Too wet, too dry, lid on, lid off . . . and so on.

When you first plant the terrarium in a lidded fish bowl, the plants will be wet and the moss misted, which may initially cause increased condensation. It is *very important* to wipe the inside of the glass walls dry with a paper towel at least once a week. During the first few days, prop the lid open a bit so you create a space for moisture to escape. Until the terrarium has a chance to attain its moisture equilibrium, you may have to watch over your new creation for a time. But that is part of learning to be an expert, yes?

Footed Glass Vessels

The difference between a footed glass vessel and a fish bowl is height. When I use this glass shape, it leads me to pick the plants that will spill out the top. This terrarium style can be a bit wilder, using plants with soft weeping leaves that go up and out, as in my Beach Life example on page 104. Plants can hug the rim of the glass and slide down the outside. You can bring a more formal look with a plant such as *Draceana marginata*, which has a stiffer leaf. It can jut out from center to tip and make a striking scene when viewed from above.

Footed glass vessels have the advantage of raising a terrarium off wherever it is sitting so you see exactly what is in the bottom. This is a consideration when you're picking drainage material. Do you want colored material to match the plant leaf shades, such as colored sand, or do you want to give it an earthy woodland feel by using bark chips at the bottom? Many terrarium designers use sheet moss. I don't usually because I am fond of material with a texture. I prefer to use moss as topdressing to finish the look. The perspective is all your choosing. After you have completed many versions, you will develop preferences. I am confident that once the terrarium bug has bitten you, you will never stop making terrariums of every variation.

LIDDED COOKIE JARS AND APOTHECARY JARS

Some of my favorite and most successful terrariums have been in lidded jars. Plants in lidded jars do not need watering, cleaning, or pruning for months at a time. Choose the proper plants, and your design will be maintenance free. Modern apothecary jar lids usually have a bit of a wiggle to them, and I believe this looser fit allows air to enter in and out, keeping the moisture level healthy for the plants. Even new apothecary jars have a vintage look, as if they came from a time long gone. They elevate what is inside them to a sophisticated status.

I have also placed larger orchids like *Phalaenopsis*, moth orchids, or *Paphiopedilum*, slipper orchids, in tall apothecary jars for display. I don't expect the orchid to live there indefinitely, so I do not actually plant it inside. Instead, I will gently drop the orchid into the glass vessel in its original pot. I then use loosely placed Spanish moss around and on the pot to hide its presence. This makes a fashionable presentation. Maybe I'll add a small fern or spidery plant alongside for accent if there is enough room. The orchid will last longer in the extra humidity. Keep your eye on the buildup of condensation; you may need to wipe out the vessel occasionally.

PARLOR TRICK

I had a small *Neanthe bella* palm in a 16-inch-tall lidded apothecary jar. These "parlor palms" were so-called during Victorian times because sitting rooms or "parlors" were poorly lit by sunlight, most likely because they were shaded by heavy velvet drapes, but still the plants survived. These parlor palms tolerate low light and neglect. I added an "ancient ruin" from an aquarium shop with a few scattered rocks that had the appearance of broken concrete from Pompeii. That terrarium went on and on and kept perfectly well for months. These elegant palms simply do not protest.

ABOVE: This Idyllic *Dicranum* moss specimen sits inside this large 1-gallon Anchor Hocking Core jar. This size jar has sustained moss quite well without any maintenance for months.

TOP: Here are three great sizes for terrarium use. This photo shows 1-gallon, ½-gallon, and ¼-gallon sizes. These jar styles are manufactured by Anchor Hocking. They are referred to as Core jars.

RIGHT: Here is preserved *Dicranum* mood moss hugging the space below a variegated creeping fig (*Ficus pumila*) and a smooth-leaved *Peperomia*.

Lidded Cookie Jars

Food containers, which at one time were used to hold flour, sugar, coffee, or cookies, are my newfound loves. At my local chain craft store, in the glass jar aisle, I found rounded Anchor Hocking lidded jars, with paper inserts inside that shared a picture of a completed terrarium with how-to instructions in three languages. (I was not surprised to find Anchor Hocking has informational how-to pages on their website too.)

My smallest jar size is compact and produces a sharp-looking garden under glass with just three or four 2-inch tropical plants. The glass jar lids have a slight movement to them and therefore allow *just enough* hot air to escape while keeping the inside comfortably warm and humid. I imagine it's much like Baton Rouge, Louisiana, on a hot summer day.

VINTAGE WARDIAN CASES

The large, beautiful Wardian case on the right cost only fifteen dollars because it had a broken pane. I proceeded to have a Tiffany glass expert replace the cracked pane at a cost of seventy-five dollars. I feel that I am still ahead because that's a great value, and I have a beautiful repurposed glass house that might have been discarded. Wardian case prices will vary depending on authenticity and windowpane intricacy.

Look for Wardian cases with a roof pane that swings open. During the plants' period of adjustment after planting, this roof pane will provide a way to release any excessive condensation. Some models have an attached metal stick to prop the window open when necessary. Do not leave the window open

CANNING JARS

Do *not* use hermetically sealing canning jars. What mostly likely is common sense to you was not to me. My first thought was that this jar will keep all the moisture inside nicely. I imagined that I would never need to do anything to maintain *this* terrarium. Well, hermetically sealed jars are for canning, pickling, and preserving food because the vacuum seal is airtight, with no air escaping or circulating. The plants in every terrarium I made rotted, got fungus, and had to be thrown out. Those canning jars now have flour, sugar, and pasta in them and are sitting on my kitchen counter, where they belong.

This multipaneled glass conservatory sits waiting for a multitude of designs.

for days because then you risk drying out the new planting too much.

When I plant this type of structure, I use larger plants. Tropical plants in 3-inch pots work well. I know they are likely to outgrow the case in time, but I prefer that the plants appear spectacular rather than minuscule. I find that, in general, plants do grow more slowly when placed in a confined space. (An exception would be *Soleirolia*, or baby tears, which—for me—burst with new growth in the case's humid air.) A lower light environment will also retard growth a bit.

I use plants that mimic those found in Victorian-age conservatories and are meant to imitate the larger glasshouses during the time period. You may want a tall plant that will rise into the peak of the house. Look for palms (*Neanthe bella*), a small weeping fig tree (*Ficus benjamina*), and maybe a small Norfolk Island pine (*Araucaria heterophylla*); all work adequately as a tall backdrop. Of course, ferns were also extremely popular during the reign of Queen Victoria.

A *Codiaeum variegatum*, croton 'Banana' variety, front and center, pointing its yellow fingers outward.

OPPOSITE: Use your Wardian case as a centerpiece for an outdoor summer dinner party on your lawn. Fill the case with flowering plants to create an extraordinary conversation piece.

In the front of a large glasshouse scenario, I would look for a plant to add color. In my Wardian case step-by-step instructions on page 84, I chose the shiny, thick, narrow leaves of *Codiaeum variegatum*, croton 'Banana' variety. Crotons like bright light and have a vertical form. They may not be a first choice as a terrarium plant because they are larger plants, but I've had good success using them in glasshouses where they have room to thrive. Crotons have strong leaves that stand upright, and their coloration is vibrant and exciting.

HANGING CERAMIC PLANTERS, GLASS GLOBES, AND TEARDROPS

With these types of terrariums, you can experiment with sizes, how high or low they are presented in your space, and the colors of the planters themselves. Hanging terrariums come in so many new shapes and sizes: the usual round

There are so many combinations to make using moss, sand, rocks, or bark chips with many different plants. Why not change them on a monthly basis for holidays and parties? The step-by-step instructions start on page 92.

RIGHT: Peer into the suspended world of air plants living on a bed of river stones high above the floor.

This is a classic use of hanging vessels.

sphere or long pear shape referred to as a teardrop. The oval pill shape (one of my favorites) is another interesting choice; one small plant will pop out the hole, or you can drop an air plant inside.

Pinterest shares pages and pages of hanging glass terrarium scenarios in homes, as window displays, suspended over dining tables like chandeliers, in restaurants, or—my favorite—as art installations.

I visited Wave Hill, a beautiful estate destination in the Bronx, New York, nestled on a precipice overlooking the Hudson River and the Palisades across the river divide. In its art gallery was featured an art installation of glass jars hanging on strings at various heights and positions in a window, capturing the light. It reminded me of the small glass spheres used to hold air plants in suspension. I immediately wanted to run home and recreate their set-up. Sadly, I have yet to find the space.

Glass Globes for Special Displays

Glass globes are extremely versatile. During the Christmas season, you can build a few hanging terrariums to hang like ornaments on your fir or spruce tree. Fill them

White sand equals fake snow! Here a row of winter snow air plant (*Tillandsia*) hanging glass globes with faux pine branch cuttings or chartreuse bits of preserved reindeer moss.

with pinecones and include minute red, green, gold, or silver glass balls plus balsam-scented potpourri. Mmmm . . . breathe in the outdoors.

The great thing with glass globes is they can hang or they can sit on a flat surface. The sitting glass globes have a flat surface on the bottom, so consider which style you want when you make your purchase. Of course, if the globe is an absolute sphere, you'll need to make sure it includes a glass ring or hook at the top to string a ribbon or length of twine through in order to suspend it.

How about creating a sensory spa experience in your bathroom with lavender? Convert your glass globes into scented terrariums with crystals or white stones. The potent aroma of lavender potpourri is believed to cause relaxation in our bodies. Different lavender varieties have their own unique aromas, so do a sniff test. Light some candles and create a place where you can unwind from our fast-paced world.

INSPIRATION FROM SOCIAL MEDIA

Check out my Resource Guide on page 165 for social media contacts; maybe you'll connect with those in your own area for supplies as well as inspiration. Social media has the power to instantly bring people together. As I researched the lavender concept, I found a mail-order supplier for this concept at a terrarium shop, Luludi, in Astoria, New York. Liza Fiorentinos, the owner, had already incorporated this idea into her style of terrarium and event décor. I tweeted Liza with my own comments. Then, in return, Liza looked me up on social media and signed up for my workshop. She walked into my life a week later. We just never know where our inspirations will come from—around the world or in the next town.

At one of my many forays into selling terrariums at street fairs, I spontaneously purchased a 4-foot-tall gardenia topiary to decorate my booth, hoping it would attract potential customers as they made their way down the avenue from booth to booth. That gardenia plant had *nothing* to do with terrariums, but it was a beautiful distraction that caused many people to share stories of front porches with gardenias blooming on long-ago summer days. The gardenia aroma became a memorial of days gone by. Splendidly for me, before the day's end, a woman purchased the floral inspiration simply because it sparked pleasant memories that pulled her to her childhood home.

Today, there are mail-order kits available so you can make your own glass globe arrangements. There is no shame in buying pre-made glass globes filled with air plants and moss or sand and succulents. These precious botanical worlds are showing up at the most unexpected businesses, such as grocery stores and fruit markets.

Why not create a small floral terrarium, even temporarily, by combining an aromatic bloom such as a gardenia with a small corresponding plant such as an elegant fern and, of course, the finishing touch, moss? Float the flowers, with their deep engaging perfume in a glass globe suspended at eye level. This is a gardenia bloom. Its aroma is intoxicating.

CLOCHE DISPLAYS AND LANTERNS

Cloches improve the display of any plant. Small terrarium displays that contain an unusual plant variety can be housed under a glass dome to create a real showcase. All my cherished specimens and treasures go under a cloche that is displayed prominently in my home. Lanterns are elegant and elevate the objects to museum pieces. The lantern is the glass container on the left in the photo on page 64. I purchased it at my local Anthropologie, and althought it's usually used to burn candles, I simply plugged up any spaces with plumber's caulk and filled it with sand and air plants. You will find instructions in Chapter 4 on page 89.

These are very different glass displays where you can create beautiful designs that are either extremely minimal or are extravagant displays of nature.

OPPOSITE: You can create a makeshift cloche by using a lid from another container that has enough space under its dome to host plants.

Cloches

A cloche dictates what sits beneath the glass by the interior size of the dome. The dictionary definition of a cloche (pronounced *klohsh*) is a bell-shaped glass cover that can be placed over a plant outside to protect it from frost and encourage growth. Cloches were primarily used in outdoor gardening to start vegetables growing in the garden before the last frost date. The sun's heat intensifies under the glass and warms the ground, protecting and encouraging seedlings to grow. Today, elegant glass versions for interior design are

SPRING BULB BLOOM TERRARIUMS

You can create a temporary terrarium cloche display in wintertime with spring-blooming bulbs, such as paperwhites or mini yellow daffodils (*Narcissus*), or delicate white snowdrops (*Galanthus* spp.) on a moss base. I buy small pots of these spring bloomers and place them on the glass pedestal in their plastic or clay pot and then surround the pot with sheet moss until I have a lovely harbinger of spring for indoors. This fresh display reminds us that the snow will thaw and flowers will rise above the soil to greet us soon.

abundantly available in most home décor retail shops or by online mail-order websites. I found a terrific wholesaler's website, www.modernvaseandgift.com, where I can view many sizes of cloches.

CAKE STANDS, COMPOTE DISHES, AND FOOTED FRUIT BOWLS

These food-serving pieces are made of sturdy, thick glass and can withstand being filled with sand or soil and plants. Even so, when you choose to use food service pieces, do consider the strength of the glass. I would not use expensive

This footed parfait bowl and the lidded cake plate were both previously used for serving food. Not anymore!

heirloom pieces for fear they would be destroyed by the weight of the terrarium ingredients.

I bought a covered cake plate to exhibit my tasteful entertaining style, but I have yet to serve cake on it (I did pile a few cupcakes into it once). When using any covered dish, keep in mind they produce more humidity and need plants that can withstand the increased dampness.

The deep space of a footed compote dish can require a great deal of soil or sand, if you fill it to the rim. I suggest that when you plant, only fill the interior with about 2 inches of planting medium. Then you can plant low in the dish and let the plants either grow up to the rim or use plants that have a horizontal growth pattern, such as a ground cover that will stay low. Succulents, such as *Echeveria*, would be a good choice too. It produces fleshy rosettes that do not grow rapidly. Work in some colored sand to create interesting layers.

These glass food service pieces are fun and different containers to use for terrariums. This photo was taken in haste but it has captured the wild arrangement of a jumble of tropical plants. There is a woody *Vinca* vine tumbling over the edge and a small *Neanthe bella* palm reaching out from the rear with a center autumn fern. This arrangement was not pre-planned or thought out and doesn't have much of a theme except "overflowing abundance."

CHAPTER 4

GETTING STARTED

I'll admit to having some apprehension before I start building a new terrarium. I have all these components—how will I accomplish the final project?

There are just a few basic steps to keep in mind on your way to success. This chapter shares the standard, traditional, classic terrarium building steps for any vessel. Familiarize yourself with these concepts, and you'll be able to adapt them to your own unique abilities, interests, plant availability, and, of course, glass terrarium vessel. I suggest that you just dive right in. There are step-by-step photos to guide you on your way.

- Assemble the ingredients.
- Choose the plants.
- Place the drainage material at the bottom.
- Add a divider to separate the planting medium from the drainage well.
- Place your activated charcoal.
- Decide where the plants will be placed.
- Plant, tamp down, and add the final potting mix.
- Topdress your final design to finish the look.

Even after creating many terrariums, I will always find it such a pleasure to watch a project start with piles of individual ingredients and end with something so special and rewarding that you can enjoy every day. Let's get going!

BASIC TERRARIUM MATERIALS

Take a look at this list of basic materials for building terrariums. Do you think something is missing? Some sources will tell you to use gloves, but I don't recommend doing that because I don't believe in using gloves—get your hands in there, and get them dirty! Your hands are two of the best tools you have available. I also don't specify a watering can in this list because those dump way too much water at one time; most people cannot control the water flow from them—even me.

- Glass vessel
- Activated charcoal
- Plants (appropriate to your design)
- Drainage material (plus divider of some sort)
- Potting mix
- Topdressing (if any)

STEP ONE: CREATE DRAINAGE

You'll need to create a drainage well at the bottom of your glass container where any excess water will drain into and gather. This is a very important component to any indoor garden project. In the outdoors, water just washes away. Your container has no such escape route!

This is the time to decide how the drainage material will affect your overall landscape design. Are you using sand? Is it a natural color or green, pink, or orange? Do you want to use bark chips as your woody moisture catch-all? Each material gives a different "feel" to the design.

You also want to decide how much room you have for the drainage area, and how much of this material you want to be able to view through the glass walls in the finished design. How large or tall is your container? Will it only hold a ¼-inch of stone, or more? If you pour too much material in the bottom, will your plants fit into the space available? Have you decided to let a few plants peek out the top?

Make your decisions before you move to the next step.

STEP TWO: CREATE THE SPACE BETWEEN DRAINAGE AND POTTING MIX

Here you can make a choice regarding the material or ingredient you want separating the drainage material from the potting mix above it. A thin barrier ensures the layered area retains its design appeal.

I like to use a paper divider because I like how it creates clear, distinct layers of separation, highlighting the drainage material and preventing the potting mix or sand from seeping into the bottom. I use a thin barrier in most of my terrarium building but, please, always experiment with different methods and materials till you find whether paper, moss, or bark works best for your designs.

I use old-fashioned brown construction paper to match the soil color. The color hides the paper from view through the glass. If you are using sand at the bottom of your design, then match the paper to the color of the sand. You can repeat this again and again if you are building multiple layers. Sometimes I want the bottom layer to stand out as part of a design's visual effect. Many terrarium designers suggest using a layer of preserved sheet moss. This is also appropriate, but it does change the look. Some folks use coffee filters or cheesecloth, both of which are permeable. You will find examples in the photos of the specific step-by-step instruction in this chapter.

Now place bits of activated charcoal on top of the barrier or separator before pouring in your potting mix. The activated charcoal will filter and purify the potting mix and absorb excess moisture, which can cause rotting. If you begin to add potting mix and forget the activated charcoal, simply add some to your potting mix and dump it all in. It's better to have a few bits of activated charcoal than none at all.

STEP THREE: PLANTING

Now you're at the planting stage. This is a very important step as you are creating your landscape.

First, lay down a layer of potting mix into which you'll place your plants. If the houseplant potting mix that I have available is somewhat dry and flyaway, I'll place the mix in a separate container (such as a bowl), spray a *slight* bit of water onto it, and mix. Do not add so much water that the soil becomes a soupy mess; it should just be moistened slightly.

You should play around with the placement of your plants outside the terrarium, just on the table or work surface. Move them around until they complement one another. You can also place them inside the empty glass vessel, if they fit easily, to check if they fit like you imagined.

Once you have your drainage level and potting mix down as a base, you can add plants. You will see right away if a plant is too tall or needs a leaf or stem to be cut off to fit inside your glass container. Maybe you'll choose to move one plant to the side for interest instead of grouping them all in the middle in a clump. Then you can experiment by adding decorative elements to make a stone path or a dry riverbed between plants.

As you pull the tiny plants out of their pots, you may see that the rootball is overgrown or too big for your terrarium. You can either root prune or cut down the size of the rootball completely. You will find a photo showing how to prune roots on page 77.

This next task is also important. Before the final placement, make sure your healthy plants are clear of dead leaves or debris. Also, give the rootballs some water by squirting them with your mister or dipping them in water. Your mister will become your most important tool while building your terrariums, as well as for maintaining your indoor gardens.

I prefer watering the plants *before* planting because you can be sure the plants have been adequately watered; it eliminates guessing. I would not add additional water to a newly planted terrarium, as moisture can accumulate so quickly. Yes, adding additional water can be detrimental, so I usually plan to ventilate the new terrarium the first day.

Terrariums are very detail focused—and tiny—so now you'll begin to use some of the specialized tools I mentioned earlier in the book. Besides household utensils, one of my favorite tools is a funnel. Once you place your plants, you do not want to inexactly pour more soil and gravel all over them. This can ruin the design and create clutter for you as you try to clean up a space into which you can barely get your fingers. (See page 32 for more details about tools.)

As I plant a terrarium, I am constantly wiping or washing my hands. If my hands are full of soil, then the plants will be messy when I install them. That we can't have! As I mentioned previously, it is harder to clean off the plants after they are in the terrarium. Sometimes I even wash the leaves of my plants if I think they are stiff or sturdy enough to stand a bit of slow-running stream of water. I would do this to plants like *Peperomia* or arrowhead. Ferns might be too delicate for washing. There should be no dead leaves or soil on your plants to muck up the beauty you see through the glass (and you know I want to say "dirt").

At this stage, add all your plants, gently tamp down the soil around the rootballs with a spoon (or possibly your fingers, if you can), and nudge the plants into place. You should make sure each plant's rootball is buried under the soil or covered with adequate amounts of moss so they will not dry out. Even in a terrarium, exposed roots can dry and can cause a plant to drop leaves and lose its shape.

If you plant well, then everything should look as if it just magically appeared together.

STEP FOUR: ADD THE TOPDRESSING

Now you can complete or decorate your terrarium. In The Basics chapter (see page 31), I established the differences between "topdressing," "design elements," and "found objects."

It is not necessary to add a bevy of objects, and maybe you don't want anything taking away from the plant design, but I do recommend including some finishing touches and covering portions of the soil. The key to stunning visual success is in the details.

Now that your plants are properly planted, look down at your design or view it through the side of the glass to find the blank areas between or around the plants. This is the spot where you'll cover the soil with moss, gravel, or bark chips, or a mix of all three.

Maybe you can add a mound of moss to place your plastic bench upon. Maybe you'll find an overhanging tropical plant limb and hide a dinosaur or frog, and allow them to peer out of the jungle you made.

Each creation begins with an empty canvas.

This step is about placement. Feel free to play with it until you find the most satisfactory outcome.

KEY DESIGN DETAILS

You just read that the key to creating your own great terrarium designs is the details. Let's talk about those details.

Go for a Variety of Plants

How do you go about deciding on the mix of plants? Sometimes it is plant availability that dictates a design. Availability will sometimes narrow my choices, but I like to use plants that will play against one another. I select plants that vary in color, leaf texture, or growth pattern, such as *Cryptanthus*, strawberry begonia, white-veined and red-veined *Fittonia*, and a small *Selaginella*, perhaps. These plants are quite varied.

Build a Basic Triangle Design

While I create a new design, I use a simple idea, the triangle.

Consider this arrangement inside your terrarium:

- Arrange plants with the tallest in the rear or in the center.
- If the tallest plant is in the rear corner, then place shorter plants in front toward the center.
- Shorter plants hide the stems of the taller plants.
- Short plants can flank the left or right corners on the outside.
- Plants at the forefront of the triangle can be groundcover or short low wide plants.
- Plants can cascade over the rim in asymmetrical glass container or open arrangements.

It helps me to keep the overall look in perspective. When planting a terrarium, I employ basic visual display or flower arranging techniques. I keep the plants close together much like a bouquet of flowers. I play the leaf textures and colors of each plant against one another. A viewer's eye will move from tall to small, darker to lighter throughout the design. (See Chapter 1, Terrarium Design, on page 15 for more on design specifics.)

STEP-BY-STEP TERRARIUM BUILDING

In this section, I'll share some of the terrariums I've created in order to teach you the basic steps of terrarium building. Once you get the hang of it, designing will seem like second nature to you, and the ideas will just flow.

- Classic Fish Bowl
- Traditional Lidded Jar
- Vintage Wardian Case
- Tillandsia Air Plant Lantern
- Hanging Ceramic Planter
- Hanging Glass Teardrop
- Classic Hanging Glass Globe
- Soilless Pebble Display
- Explorer's Still Life Cloche
- Beach Life Terrarium

The geometry of each windowpane in this lantern led to the exact placement of the elements inside. Simple and elegant seemed to work best.

CLASSIC FISH BOWL

1

INGREDIENTS

PLANTS
Fittonia, Aralia, Pilea, spider plant (*Chlorophytum comosum*)

BASICS
Activated charcoal, pea gravel, potting mix with scoop

MOSS
Sheet moss (*Hypnum*)

2

1. Building a terrarium is like baking a cake. Lay out the ingredients you need to build your design, and all will go smoothly. The building can be even easier if you use small containers to hold your ingredients. That allows you to keep one hand free to hold the plant while your other hand adds an ingredient.

2. I have chosen a piece of blue construction paper for my divider because that was literally the color that I had available. Utilize the best tools that you have available to you. The paper divider will be covered with soil and will not be visible when the terrarium is completed, so the color is not so crucial in this example. I added some activated charcoal at this step also.

3. This is a perfect example of how my plastic container full of potting mix and clear plastic scoop help me to easily dump potting mix inside. I *love* my toolkit!

4. This small *Aralia*, edged with cream-colored leaves, is a bit tall, so I cut the rootball down a bit so the plant will sit lower in the planting area. You must make an assessment each time on how much of the rootball to remove. Place the plant in the terrarium to estimate what needs to be done. It is better to be conservative and cut a little off first; you can always prune more off more if needed. Keep some of the roots complete and intact. The plants will grow new roots as they establish in their new glass home.

5. As you build up the planting area, don't be afraid to get your fingers all the way down to the soil level and nudge your plants firmly into place. This is a good way to tamp down the rootball and soil. A long-handled spoon (like an iced tea spoon) is *perfect* for tamping down soil. Use its curved, smooth bottom. This tool can reach farther down into your terrarium than your fingers might. Whether you use your hands or tools is determined by you and your comfort level.

6

6. After adding some additional potting mix around the inside perimeter, I got soil on the inside glass walls. A simple hit to the glass with a few squirts of water cleaned that right off. This also helps to moisten the dry soil, making it easier to tamp down.

7. I turned the nozzle head to mist my preserved sheet moss before placing it around the plants. You can mist both the top and bottom of your moss.

8. I have now added plants, potting mix, moss, and additional pea gravel around the edges so you can really see the design coming together. I also clean debris off the inside of the glass with a soft paper towel. This is a good practice when you need to wipe out excess condensation in any terrarium, especially lidded fish bowls.

9. I had spaces between the moss pieces, so I decided that black pebbles will show up nicely against the green moss and the earth tones of the pea gravel. I formed my hand in a scoop shape, then turned the back of my hand away from the plants, then simply let the pebbles slide down my fingers into the right spot.

10. I added a baby spider plant cutting that I'd rooted in water. It adds a great accent and texture to the array. You can't beat free plants! *Voilà!*

TRADITIONAL LIDDED JAR

INGREDIENTS

PLANTS
Creeping fig (*Ficus pumila*),
Neanthe bella palm,
Peperomia, arrowhead
(*Nephthytis*)

BASICS
Houseplant potting mix,
green craft sand, activated
charcoal

MOSS
Spanish, reindeer, mood moss
chunks

1. This jar can hold a few more plants than the fish bowl. I'll also add several bits of different moss for color and texture, as well as some matching sand.

2. Using green sand as the drainage area will complement the chartreuse moss topdressing. If I pour the craft sand directly from the cup, its fine crystals will bounce and stick to the sides of the glass. My long-nosed funnel is the perfect tool for this step.

3. I am able to place one hand on the side of the *Peperomia* to scrunch the two plants closer together. It appears that I am rough on the plants, but my movements are slow, gentle, and deliberate.

4. I begin placing the plants inside the jar, but I turn the creeping fig on its side so its variegated leaves are facing the glass wall. This technique can be used with many plants that grow upright but will be viewed through the side walls.

5. I use this larger-neck funnel because the potting mix has larger bits. There is no area open to scoop soil into the crowded jar without messing up the plants. It is easier to use a tool.

6. I have already added mood moss into this lidded jar. I prefer to tear the Spanish moss instead of cutting off pieces. It gives it a looser, more natural appearance.

7. With one hand, I gently move the creeping fig to the side while slipping in the Spanish moss with two fingers. Nimble fingers and moderate movements do not disturb what is already planted.

8. It's easier to use a stick to place this reindeer moss bit inside because it does not have fine hairlike strands like Spanish moss; it moves more freely in one piece. I am using a short, green stake that earlier was holding up another potted plant—a tool of opportunity and free of charge.

9. Here is the finished design ready to be covered and enjoyed. I watered the plants already, so no additional watering is needed for many weeks, maybe months.

VINTAGE WARDIAN CASE

INGREDIENTS

PLANTS
Creeping fig (*Ficus pumila*), *Neanthe bella* palm, croton (*Codiaeum*), ruffle fern (*Nephrolepis exaltata*), club moss (*Selaginella kraussiana*)

BASICS
Houseplant potting mix, activated charcoal

MOSS
Dicranum, living mounds of mood moss

1. The glasshouse lids of many Wardian-style terrariums tower above a low tray. You can change your technique accordingly to accommodate the shallow planting dish. I placed the potted plants inside the case to try out their position before actually planting.

2. I'm ready to begin the building process, section by section. I start in the center, then move around the tallest palm tree to create a tropical jungle.

3. I did not create a foundation of soil in this model for the plants to sit upon. The plants will sit directly at the bottom of the tray, and I'll trim their rootballs as needed (as described in the Classic Fish Bowl project). I build plant by plant, according to the placement I laid out in the test run.

4. I want to keep a shallow depth of potting mix. But I need a larger quantity of potting mix to fill this larger tray so dumping soil right from the container seems faster. At this stage, you can add some activated charcoal.

WARDIAN CASE BARRIERS

There will be no paper barrier, moss separator, or any drainage material in this Wardian case planting tray. We will have to plant directly into the tray; it simply is too shallow otherwise. After a Wardian case is planted, its watering schedule will most likely be infrequent to almost never because the glass roof will hold moisture inside. In a six-month period, it will need *some* water; the amount depends on how much moisture escapes through the roof window and how warm the room is where this glass house is located. Environmental factors affect the final care considerations.

5. I always like to moisten the soil slightly and tamp down around the rootballs so each plant stays in place. I use only one or two sprays to dampen potting mix if needed, then press the soil down to keep plants in place.

6. I continue building around the center plants and filling in the outer viewing areas. This *Selaginella* is quite fluffy, and its branching hangs in the air nicely.

7. I added smaller plants at the base to act as groundcover around the larger plants. They will grow and fill in the landscape. You can allow the creeping fig vine to encircle the entire base if that is your preference. It will grow slowly over time, but its tendrils will elongate eventually. You should snip the vine's ends from time to time, which will encourage healthy growth and help create thicker stems.

8. I begin to add a large mound of mood moss to cover all the soil areas. I support the moss section gingerly in my palm, holding it flat so it won't crumble.

9. I hold the plants back and slide the whole moss mound into the corner. It will look like a rich, soft ground surface, and the vine can crawl over it as it lengthens.

10. Take a close look at how the plants sit against one another. The *Selanginella* floats above the moss floor.

11

11. The finished Wardian case looks much like the original placement in step one, but now the plants are settled in and ready to lay down roots in their new glass home.

TILLANDSIA AIR PLANT LANTERN

INGREDIENTS

PLANTS
Air plants (*Tillandsia*),
Cryptanthus

BASICS
Gray floral supply sand,
two large granite stones

1. This is an elegant assortment of ingredients. In any particular design, you may not use everything you have assembled. Sometimes as you build a design, you'll get to the point where you say, "This is done."

2. I am using my favorite funnel to pour the sand inside the lantern. The lantern is large, and I want to keep the sand from bouncing up from the bottom. As the sand pours, I stop and shake the lantern slightly to level out the sand. Then I look at the front of the lantern from the outside to see if the amount of sand is visible through the glass.

3. I literally ran outside to find this rock. I wanted something sizable to sit the air plant on, but I must place it carefully so it does not damage the glass. This display cannot be moved once it's completed.

4. After moving the plant around, I settled on this spot because it looked as if it grew there. I can also view it through the side windowpane. Yes, I *am* this determined to find just the right spot. The completed creation will show that the effort is worth it.

5. I gingerly added a second, small, whiter stone with black speckles to coordinate with the fine floral sand. Then I added a second air plant to the rear as a backdrop because it will reach above the opening. The two small identical *Cryptanthus* were not used in the final arrangement. They would have crowded the perfect simplicity of this design.

6. The completed terrarium is an attractive natural collection of unique natural things. As my eyes rest on each object inside, moving from plant to stone, I feel very serene.

HANGING CERAMIC PLANTER

INGREDIENTS

PLANTS
Peperomia varieties

BASICS
Pea gravel, houseplant potting mix with scoop, activated charcoal, loose natural pebbles, builder's sand

MOSS
Sheet moss

1. Hanging ceramic planters, glass globes, or teardrops come in so many variations. Here are three basic shapes alongside their tiny plants, each just waiting to climb inside.

2. The bluebird egg-colored hanging planter needs a base of pea gravel.

3. My scoop is the perfect size to slide some houseplant potting mix over the pea gravel. I placed a small wad of sheet moss over the gravel to separate it from the soil with a piece or two of activated charcoal for good health.

4. I use my beloved *Peperomia* again. You should always check to see if there is enough soil inside for the plant to sit at the height you want; if there's not, take the plant out and add or remove soil.

5. I like how this *Peperomia* will peek out the top and keep its shape, but its growth pattern is challenging for this container. It grows fast! You can try a cascading plant if you like a draping effect. Plant choice is based on how the plant's structure holds itself up or how it naturally weeps downward.

HANGING GLASS TEARDROP

INGREDIENTS

PLANTS
Haworthia

BASICS
Pea gravel, loose natural
pebbles, builder's sand

MOSS
Colored Spanish moss

1. Using a scoop filled with builder's
sand, I tilt the glass teardrop to pour a
level amount of sand at the bottom.

2. I tilt the plant this time and move
it in top first. The small *Haworthia*
succulent has an architectural and
vertical form. It may not live here
forever, but it is darling right now.

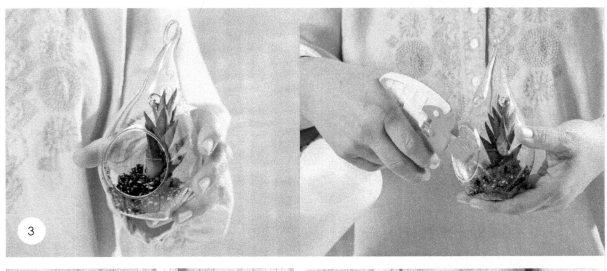

3. This *Haworthia* is sitting pretty. I make sure it has some water before it is buried.

4. I can either cover the rootball with cactus potting mix or sand. I want to keep with the true desert look of the plant, so I go with the dry sand.

5. Always decorate in the final phase. Here I'm using some natural pebbles to continue the desert-themed landscape.

6. I think this tiny world needs one more touch to fill the empty space on the left side. I grab a scrap of lime green Spanish moss and poke it in.

7. Now I am satisfied the tiny world is balanced and has variety.

CLASSIC HANGING GLASS GLOBE

INGREDIENTS

PLANTS
Gasteria

BASICS
Pea gravel, loose natural
pebbles, builder's sand

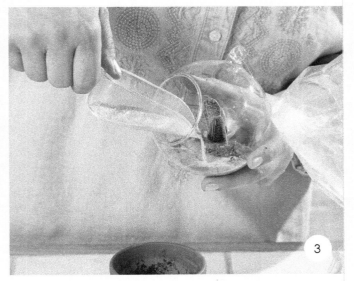

1. Up next is this darling small glass globe. I have more sand and would like to hang this with the hanging teardrop terrarium in the previous example to create a theme.

2. You'll notice that this plant is stripped of potting mix from its original pot and placed in the terrarium almost bare-rooted. Eventually, those roots will expand into the new potting medium and take hold.

3. I bury the loose roots of this *Gasteria* succulent in sand. It will need topdressing because the plant is so small and isolated in the globe.

4. I add small river stones because they vary in color. Also, their size is smaller and I can fit more of them inside the globe.

5. This is a simple arrangement, but at the same time it's suitable and cute.

6. The happy hanging terrarium triad—the round sphere glass globe, oval blue ceramic planter, and pear-shaped teardrop—is ready to hang up anywhere!

SOILLESS PEBBLE DISPLAY

1. This is a simple project that shows how to layer different size stones to enhance a small container. The glass also has vertical ridges that catch the light. I am very fond of this small tower of succulents and stone. It sits on my bookcase in an east-facing window where it can bathe in the morning sun.

2. I use paper dividers to keep materials separate and distinct. This project does not need a divider between the aquarium gravel and the river stones to keep them separate, but I add one between the layers because soil will also be added around the rootball of our small *Haworthia*. The potting mix tends to slide through stone and will ruin a layered arrangement.

INGREDIENTS

PLANTS
Haworthia, jade plant
(*Crassula* species)

BASICS
Aquarium gravel, river stones, pea gravel topping, paper divider

3. As I hold the tiny succulent near its destination in the glass cylinder, I use a plastic spoon to scoop out the plant and potting mix from its original plastic pot. I want the plant's rootball surrounded by soil in the glass cylinder so that soil will retain water to nourish the plants, even though the *Haworthia* and jade plant will be buried in stones at completion.

4. I use a tool, the white plastic spoon, because the small rootball is falling apart, and I need to get it into the narrow cylinder opening as quickly and as intact as possible. I anchor the roots in the soil as I tenderly hold the tip of the leaves, being very careful not to break them.

5. I place a tiny jade plant behind the *Haworthia* but I raise it up a bit on some stones so that it towers slightly above the other plant. The final step is to fill in around the plants with some pea gravel that has a slightly different but natural color. I use my hand, angled like a scoop, to direct the pebbles.

6

7

6. Peering into the top to see the faces of the duo looking up. I adore them—their symmetry, their structure, their placement.

7. I fall in love with my projects and don't want to give them away. Mine, all mine!

EXPLORER'S STILL LIFE CLOCHE

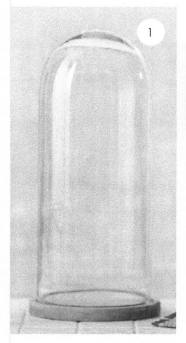

INGREDIENTS

PLANTS
Staghorn fern (*Platycerium grande*) with roots wrapped in sheet moss (Kokedama-style, see page 143)

BASICS
Marsh reeds, framed butterfly (*Delias hyparete*), willow twigs, moss ball, silk grass

1. These beginnings are like a blank canvas, full of opportunity for originality. The cloche with the wooden base requires a pot inside to contain potting mix or moss for a small garden collection. You can use only one pot.

2. This approach takes a steady hand and a firm grip on the tall glass cover. You must hold it carefully as you tilt the top sideways. Your other hand will move the plant or potted collection up into the dome. In this photo, I am adding reeds after I had already placed the staghorn fern (*Platycerium grande*) inside. The fern would have been enough by itself, a likely explorer's specimen, but I added another natural element—marsh reeds. You could consider this design complete in its simplicity.

3. I continue, though, by adding a red silk poppy with a golden yellow center. I also stabbed a few willow twigs into my moss ball to keep it near the top of the dome. The cloche design is starting to fill up at the rooftop. In this stage, it's a pretty picture as an arrangement of natural life. Should we stop at this stage?

4

4. This final addition was a challenge. I had to enlist the help of another pair of hands. Lori Adams, my photographer, slid the glass dome straight up about 2 inches (not sideways) while I placed the Painted Jezebel butterfly on a wooden pedestal. I added a bunch of silk grass (not real grass) and tucked in the forefront of the moss rootball. I tried placing the butterfly without the wooden block underneath, but it did not fall into the optimum spot for viewing through its glass frame. When we lifted the winged creature an extra inch, we could see the fronds of the fern, which created a focal point right at the opening of the wings. The two bottom yellow wings lay against the dark green background of the moss ball. Your eyes flutter right to it. The red poppy bloom picks up the slight tint of red in its wings. Everything *is* in the details, exactly presented.

BEACH LIFE TERRARIUM

INGREDIENTS

PLANTS
Ponytail palm (*Beaucarnea recurvata*)

BASICS
Builder's sand, pea gravel, wooden and wire fence, seashells

This is the view of the bay off Cape Cod, Massachusetts. The dune grasses grow out of the sand hill, and you walk down the steep wooden steps to the sand where you meet the zigzag beach fence.

1. The start of every great terrarium begins with drainage medium. This time I am using printer paper as my divider, covering the drainage area completely. It is strong and will hold up against the weight of the sand.

2. The paper helps keep the planting medium out of the drainage area, but it also helps keep the planting area a bit drier by keeping excess moisture away from the planting mixture. In this design, I used only sand for the effect, not as a drainage medium. (It is not actually beach sand.)

3. This plant is much larger than I originally thought it should be. Pony tail palms can be found in smaller pot sizes. What should you do if the size you want isn't available? Let me show how you can use this rootbound plant.

4. I begin to pull this poor plant apart. Plants can tolerate some dismantling. I pull gently and try not to tear the roots, but only untangle them. A ponytail palm can tolerate short periods of drought, so it's better to plant it in a sandy, quick-drying planting medium than in moist potting mix.

5. I am going to use only a portion of the original plant because the entire plant is just too large. Even so, the palm is rather tall and will hang out over the edges of the glass.

6. I give the roots a dunk. Always give your plants a drink before planting. Do not add or pour any additional water into the completed terrarium—things get too wet too fast—and you will know for sure that the roots have had an adequate drink. When planting in sand, water drains away.

7. I've kept the fan leaf pattern with the blush of pink forward. This plant has a pretty way of growing up and outward. When you are planting, look at your plants and turn them around and around until you find the side with the best leaves and branching. This will help with the overall design of the final project.

8. I added more pea gravel around the edges of the glass and buried the rootballs in sand. Now the pea gravel material is part of the design and seen from outside with the sand atop of it.

9. I accidently buried the rootballs too deep; I could no longer see the interesting branching fan pattern. So I used a brush to clear away the sand with a quick sweep.

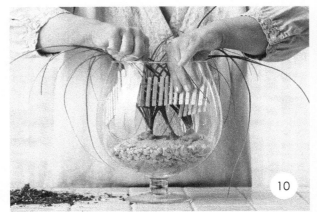

10. I had to roll up the fence outside of the glass in order to get it inside, then I had to curl it again inside. I bent the wires to give it a more typical beach fence look; those fences are never straight from fighting the tides. I add a few shells from my collection. Now I feel like I'm back on Cape Cod.

11. I grew up in New York State and spent my summers running on the beaches of Jones Beach State Park on the Atlantic Ocean. One of my many memories was of the site of the wooden fence along the entrance to the beach where the dune grasses grow. You knew you were finally at the beach when you ran past the fences and dug your toes into the hot sand! This small terrarium is my tribute to all the days past (and future) spent dreaming of beach life.

I hope that you feel completely ready now to tackle your own terrarium building after seeing examples of different building techniques in different types of glass vessels. You have learned that it is possible to use no potting mix with some plants and how a closed terrarium may not need your care for months. You have learned how the basic ingredients are incorporated one step at a time to create a miniature garden under glass. I am very excited for you to get started using your own ideas. Enjoy!

CHAPTER 5

THE PLANTS

This chapter contains a special listing of specific plants that survive well in the special conditions of glass biospheres. Each creates an unique look. Some have unusual growing patterns, red veins running through their leaves, or other intriguing attributes. Others need no soil at all, just a weekly water-bath dunking.

These are the plants that I have found to best dress up terrariums while surviving the effects of warmth, humidity, and cramped living quarters. Most are houseplants that we are accustomed to seeing in pots on a windowsill or in container gardening. Terrarium plants include tropical plants, succulents, a few cacti, ferns galore, and some other very unique specimens.

Here is a list of the best terrarium and modern indoor gardening plants:

- Air plants   *Tillandsia*
- Staghorn fern   *Platycerium grande*
- Pink star   *Cryptanthus*
- Club moss   *Selaginella*
- Mexican rose   *Echeveria*
- Baby tears   *Helxine soleirolii*
- Mikado   *Syngonanthus chrysanthus*
- Creeping fig   *Ficus pumila*

What follows is a detailed plant guide that shares specifics on these great terrarium plants. I learned about these terrific plants from creating terrarium after terrarium. Now I share them with you.

INSIDER TIPS: AIR PLANT CARE

Nancy Frame is with Plantaflor USA, California (www.plantaflor.com), an air plant grower.

Do you have favorite air plants?

I have so many favorite plants: *Tillandsia tectorum*, *T. xerographica*, and *T. houston*, and all the little *T. ionantha* are small, cute, and affordable.

How do you suggest readers use air plants?

Air plants can be used in glass terrariums, attached to wood, used in sea urchins, shells, and any medium that you can find; just never use soil when creating this art. You can use sand, sea glass, moss, pebbles, and wood frames. Frames are a great way to display the plants as art for outdoor or indoor spaces. It is a great way to show off plants as wall art.

For air plants to remain living in a terrarium, we suggest consistent watering but not overwatering. You should allow the plant to adapt to its new environment. The plants do not re-bloom; however, blooming flowers can last up to two weeks. The air plants can live a long life as they produce pups and create a whole new plant or plants.

AIR PLANTS (*TILLANDSIA*)

Let's talk about air plants. Why? Because they are *fascinating*!

An air plant is an epiphyte—that is, a plant that grows non-parasitically upon a host tree, high in the rainforest canopy where there is more sun, air circulation, and moisture from rain. These plants have advantages over plants that are restricted to the ground. In the wild, air plants collect rainwater in the gaps in their leaves radiating from the center of the plant.

Their soilless habit is why we call them *air plants*—it is not because they need nothing but air to survive. Air plants need water, sun, and care just like every living thing on our planet. They need to be dunked in a water bath at least twice weekly. Why? Air plants are covered with scales that absorb water. The constant exposure to wind and heat dries them off quickly in the natural world.

Tillandsia species can take bright light, but on cloudy winter days in the Northeast, more direct sunlight is suggested. Silvery gray *Tillandsia* will tolerate sunlight, so I have mine on a window ledge to catch the setting sun, sitting behind a potted plant that provides some protection. If you want to tuck your *Tillandsia* outdoors in summer under a shady tree, just remember they will need more frequent soakings.

Tillandsia Like It Dry

Air plants work best when they're planted in open containers. They can be well-maintained on a bed of sand because when you mist the plant, which you must do occasionally, the excess water drips into

Fabiane Mandarino, a terrarium designer in Rio de Janeiro, Brazil, has brilliantly set two darling meerkats in a sand-based terrarium with air plants and wood. The sand absorbs excess water away from the air plants and keeps them nice and dry, which is just how they like it. Perfecto!

TOP: You can see how different each of these three air plants are. Imagine how different many hundreds can be!

LEFT: As part of San Francisco's Golden Gate Park Academy of Sciences rainforest exhibit, these air plants live perched on a branch as they would normally be found in their native habitat.

the sand where it is absorbed, leaving the plant itself somewhat dry. I suggest you air-dry a *Tillandsia* after watering it. Shake off some of the excess water and place the air plant on a paper towel before returning it to the terrarium.

The basic care for *Tillandsia* is:

- Bright light, but do not expose to hot, all-day sun
- Soak twice a week, minimum, if not planted in a container
- Mist three to four times per week if they're living in a glass globe *or* take out of container and soak twice per week
- Dry on paper towels with plenty of air circulation

If you're using your air plants under a cloche on a wood branch with decorative moss, for example, think of it as a short-term display. If the air plant disintegrates in time, you can replace it or change the display.

A staghorn fern appears in the Explorer's Still Life Cloche step-by-step example on page 102.

STAGHORN FERN

Platycerium grande really *is* grand! Staghorn ferns are *epiphytic*—that is, they live high in the treetops, much like orchids and air plants, and absorb moisture from the air. Even though they live in trees, they have the tree's protective canopy above, so we, too, must provide dappled light to mimic their natural environment.

Staghorn ferns have remarkable antler-like fronds. There are basically two different types of fronds (the leaf-like parts of a fern), namely the fertile green fronds and the sterile brown fronds. The green fronds, which look like the stag horns, grow spores on the undersides at the tips for reproduction. The brown fronds are green initially and, with age, turn brown, flat, and round, creating the base for the fronds to grow upon. They have protective fuzz on their leaves (which should not be removed).

Staghorn ferns are perfect for Kokedama, which is Japanese string gardening. You can read about this in the Modern Indoor Gardening chapter on page 133.

CRYPTANTHUS

I love *Cryptanthus*. It's one of my favorite plants to use in terrarium making. Why? You only need *one* to create a dynamic focal point. They are sturdy, colorful, and eye-catching. They love humidity, moisture, and warmth, which terrarium life brings. *Cryptanthus* are terrestrial bromeliads; terrestrial bromeliads live in the ground and not in the trees like most bromeliads, *Tillandsia*, or orchids that are epiphytes.

I have a green *Cryptanthus* that has existed for years in a closed-up cookie jar. Even as it grows larger, it stays colorful and resilient. And that's a perfect terrarium plant.

Another *Cryptanthus* living in a clay pot on my windowsill increases its pigmentation with the long hours of summer sun. During shorter winter days, it grows a bit paler.

FERNS

My most-desired fern is the blue-gray *Phlebodium aureum*, or blue star fern. There is also the *P. aureum mandaianum*, or bear's claw. It is lovely, too, with fingerlike, hanging fronds. Blue star fern is an epiphytic fern native to the Americas, but *P. aureum* is the only species found in North America.

Phlebodium, over many months' time, can outgrow your terrarium, but you can say that of many other plants as well. If you start with a very small plant, then the time you have together will be significant.

Dwarf holly fern (*Cyrtomium fortunei*) has tremendous style in its leaf form. The shape of each leaf petal growing opposite one another on a frond's

ABOVE: You cannot deny the strong attraction as your eye is pulled to the glorious *Cryptanthus* focal point.

TOP: *Cryptanthus* sitting in a patch of *Selaginella* in an open terrarium.

BLUE STAR FERN CARE

In a terrarium that sweats profusely, such as a lidded fish bowl, the blue star fern can develop blackened leaves from lack of air circulation and from water sitting on its fronds. Keep an eye on your terrarium, wipe out excess water with a paper towel, and gently blot the fern fronds.

ABOVE: This is the most unbelievable vertical wall planting to see, touch, and experience in person. It's a magnificent creation, located at Longwood Gardens, in Kennett Square, Pennsylvania. There must be *hundreds* of ferns and philodendron in this planting. The designer's brilliance is in the fern choices for the plant collection. Ferns encompass so many different shades of green, textures, and movement capabilities, especially in suspension, that the final scene is a work of art.

INSET: As I began to create more intricate designs for terrariums, I wanted *Phlebodium aureum*, or blue star fern, front and center. It is so majestic!

RIGHT: Holly fern (*Cytomium fortune*) is an interesting fern. It has taut, pointed leaflets growing off a central stem from a center point of the plant. This gives the fern a dramatic style, less delicate than the maidenhair fern and less textural than the Boston fern. Use this growth pattern to your advantage and sit it center stage in your design. Remember to keep the holly fern moist, or plant it in a closed glass container. This will keep the fern green and thriving.

stem is terrific. Holly fern fills out spots nicely. I find that, in pots, this fern needs to stay evenly moist or it will wilt and lose portions of its fronds. But like the blue star fern, you must prevent droplets of water from sitting on holly fern fronds: water will cause the fronds to wilt or rot.

Korean rock fern (*Polystichum tsus-simense*) is a fern I use quite often. It has that woodland look with stiff green fronds like those that grow under the trees in a forest. It also stands up to terrarium environments terrifically well.

Boston fern (*Nephrolepis exaltata* 'Duffy') is a dwarf variety of Boston fern. Boston ferns are known for shedding leaf fronds if they brown or dry, but their beauty makes the mess worth the clean-up. Perform regular checks and remove all fronds that have wilted or dropped to the floor of your terrarium.

Button fern (*Pellaea rotundifolia*) has deep green, tiny, round button leaves on a string of a stem that originates from the center of the plant on an arching arm. Button ferns are good terrarium choices because their rootballs can be tucked into a corner while their arching branches hang delicately over the other plants in the design. They hold up well to the humidity because their leaves are thick and sturdy.

Autumn fern (*Dryopteris erythrosora*) is a true woodland-looking fern, just like the ones you would step over on your walk among the trees.

Heart fern (*Hemionitis arifolia*) is a hardy leaf fern. The dark green leaf is flat and heart-shaped, and it fills out the area it occupies. Heart fern's fronds can yellow if the plant dries out, not a good outcome because the fern will lose its fullness over time. But a closed, lidded

ABOVE: In a woodland-styled terrarium, this autumn fern's *Dryopteris erythrosora* structure is different from the other plants and pops up above the moss.

TOP: Lemon button fern (*Nephrolepis cordifolia*) has a paler green color than roundleaf fern (*Pellaea rotundifolia*) but still makes for a good terrarium plant.

MIDDLE: Autumn fern (*Dryopteris erythrosora*) is a great choice for woodland forest fern terrarium designs. The fronds mimic larger versions growing in the forest in rock outcroppings and along trickling steams. *Dryopteris* likes the humidity too!

ABOVE: Bird's nest fern (*Asplenium nidus*), besides having a great common name, also has very sturdy leaf growth. The bird's nest reference is to how the fronds unfurl from a center sprouting point. This center should be kept moist with a mist of water if your terrarium is open so the fronds open properly.

FERNS I DO *NOT* USE

Is there any fern that I do not use? I do not like to use delicate varieties such as ruffle fern (*Nephrolepis exalta* 'Ruffles') or maidenhair fern (*Adiantum*). Despite the love of moisture most ferns have, I find the fronds of these two genera do not hold up under the intensity of a humid, closed environment. They lose their beauty over time. Trial and error has proven that for me.

ABOVE: The maidenhair fern (*Adiantum*) is the loveliest fern, no dispute here. In pots, they are challenging to keep alive. They are intolerant of dry air, drought, or forgetful caretakers.

terrarium can be a good place for heart fern to live so it stays moist consistently.

Bird's nest fern (*Asplenium nidus*) is terrific! This plant grows from a central hub and unfurls its leaves upward. If you can find a starter plant that will fit in your terrarium, then use it. It is a good strong contender for use in gardens under glass.

SELAGINELLA

Selaginella, commonly called club moss, is one of my favorite types of plants and one of the most challenging to maintain. I have mastered some varieties and figured out appropriate living spaces. I still have more to learn about these *very* old plants, part of an ancient group of plants whose origins can be traced back 400 million years. Moss is one of those living things, like algae, that have been on Earth since the beginning of life.

A *Selaginella* needs what I would consider contradictory conditions. They love humidity, but they need air circulation. They love a good watering, but need the soil to dry out ever so slightly before watering again. They need to take a breath of fresh air. It is enough to make even the most eager botanist lose patience. The upside is that the right glass shape can be the solution and can, of course, reveal the beauty of the plant itself.

A few other moss plants that do well in terrariums are Irish moss (*Sagina subulata*) is a groundcover you can plant outdoors in your garden in Zones 4 to 9. It tucks neatly into corners and is evergreen in warm environments. It will hold up in open terrariums as long as you don't roast it in the summer heat.

MARIA'S FAVORITE *SELAGINELLA* PLANTS

There are different species and varieties and they have a slightly different leaf structure from one another.

Selaginella kraussiana 'Aurea'
Common favorite used in terrariums; has a stiff branching finger pattern; bright color.

Selaginella kraussiana brownii 'Emerald Isle'
Very compact variety that creates a green mat; can be used in tiny terrariums.

Selaginella kraussiana 'Gold Tips'
Yet another variation on the favorite; its new growth is lighter at the tips.

Selaginella martensii 'Frosty Fern'
Available in the winter holiday season for its appearance of fallen snow upon its tips; really lovely.

Selaginella moellendorffii
Soft texture; dark green; used in terrarium and bonsai; tolerates cooler temperatures.

Selaginella pallescens
Fine foliage; lighter green; good terrarium plant; can hold up droplets of condensation; slow grower.

Selaginella plana
Strong upright branching; able to achieve more growth height; creates elegant effect in Wardian cases.

Selaginella erythropus
Red, sometimes bronze mahogany tone; short branches; slow to grow; avoid extreme heat.

Selaginella uncinata
Long arching branches; 'Peacock' has a blue iridescence; can grow large.

Selaginella flabellata
Flat branching; feels and looks a bit coarser; another branching finger pattern.

Here is the club moss (*Selaginella kraussiana* 'Aurea') in classic green and lime green.

INSIDER TIPS: ITTIE BITTIE™ PLANTS

Kelley Howard is the owner and creator of Enviro-Cakes, the mail-order division of Batson's Foliage Group in Mt. Dora, Florida (www.batsononline.com/ittie-bitties-2). This company grows plants especially for the fairy garden and terrarium world.

How and why did you start Enviro-Cakes?

When the popularity of terrariums began, we used the plants that we developed in our wholesale business and called them Ittie Bitties™. We used the mini-plants to build a terrarium in a glass cake plate that you would normally use to serve dessert. We called that item an Enviro-Cake. We thought it would be a popular item and promoted it on our website. Enviro-Cakes was born!

Do you have a few favorites that you recommend to readers for their growth, strength, and attractive looks?

While we grow a wide variety of Ittie Bitties™ for our mixes, we do have some favorites. The *Neanthe bella* palms, and *Fittonia* and *Peperomia* plants all make excellent terrarium plants. They *love* a terrarium environment and really thrive. The palms give a tall element to your design, the *Fittonia* give a creeping look, and the *Peperomia* come in all colors and textures, but tend to lean toward a bushy look that performs well when pruned. Care is minimal on all of these, even outside a terrarium as houseplants, which make them great candidates for an open or closed scenario. I am a big fan of all plants that will take my abuse. I constantly forget to water at home—yes, me too—and these varieties are always forgiving.

Is there any type of maintenance technique you suggest once they are in a terrarium?

Incorporated in a closed terrarium, these plants should take care of themselves by creating their own ecosystem, as all closed terrariums do. It is important when building a closed terrarium to avoid overplanting it, so create a design that includes plants, mosses, and rocks to fill the space. The growth of the plants will be naturally regulated but, if the growth becomes too heavy, it can always be trimmed back to maintain the size wanted. It's the same thing that happens with a bonsai. Trim to make the plants fatter and stronger.

SUCCULENTS

How beautiful is a succulent? Their magnificent beauty is amazing and judging by their present-day popularity, many agree.

Echeveria is a large genus of succulent plants native to semi-desert areas in the Americas. A fun fact: this genus was named after the eighteenth-century

Mexican botanical artist Atanasio Echeverría y Godoy (1763–1819). His explorations took him all over documenting the beautiful rosette form of this desert dweller.

Succulents benefit from regular deep watering and fertilizing but need to dry out between watering. What does regular "deep watering" mean? Every seven to ten days, I take my small pots of succulents and pour a few ounces of water into the pots, then wait until they drip-drain *completely* before returning them to their sunny spot.

You can adapt this deep watering technique to terrariums by setting your mister on stream and targeting the *rootball* with a few well-directed blasts of water. After that, let the succulents have their drying-out period.

If succulents dry out severely, they may lose their lower leaves. This is why I tend over them like a doting parent. If I miss a watering cycle and find a dead leaf hiding under the rosette, I pull it off with a tweezers. If a succulent leaf breaks off, and as a result, a plant loses its attractive, compact appearance, it may need to be re-rooted or

Succulents and cacti are unique plants that easily beautify our life. Create your own collection in a sunny room.

TOP RIGHT: Here is a favorite open bowl design with red club moss, *Selaginella erythropus* 'Sanguinea'. Its underside matches the blood-red veins of the *Fittonia*.

TOP LEFT: After planting this open-footed brandy glass with two *Dracaena* plants—one a spiked *D. marginata* and other a lime green-striped *D. reflexa*—filling it to capacity, tuck a small *Selaginella kraussiana* 'Aurea' on the side wall. The gold club moss begins to expand as if it's finally found its long lost pals. The shape of its new home creates the ideal combination of moisture and air circulation.

ABOVE: Here's a sweet pebble terrarium for your desk, bookcase, or kitchen counter. Squirt a few bursts of water into the roots every few weeks. While some succulents grow rapidly, these are some that sit quietly in a small world and impress us with endless delight. The different stone colors and sizes are also captivating.

TOP: Succulents galore, marching to your front door. All in a row, they are just so gorgeous and fabulous!

MIDDLE: *Echeveria* has the beautiful rosette form of the succulent world. Its colors vary from soft green to a pale blue hue. Everyone loves *Echeveria*; we simply cannot resist them.

MIDDLE RIGHT: Even in the cold winter snow, tongue plant (*Gasteria pillansii*), jade (*Crassula ovuta*), and zebra plant (*Haworthia attenuate* var. *raduta*) are warm inside their glass home.

RIGHT: These cedar-frame boxes look complex with all those spaces to fill, but succulents, especially hens and chicks, will grow and fill in quickly. This vertical garden succulent box is a planter that allows you to grow a hanging garden with little effort.

propagated. If dead leaves are not removed, they may decay, harboring fungus that can then infect the plant.

Some groups of succulents can grow at an alarming rate. I bought a small succulent that I believe now was *Kalanchoe thyrsiflora* and, in a few short months, it *tripled* in height. As magnificent as it had become, I could not house it in a terrarium.

Spotted penwiper plant (*Kalanchoe marmorata*) is also very lovely, but it will grow quickly. If you actually are able to buy one of these amazing specimens, just know that its terrarium life will be short-lived, and the plant will be on display in a terrarium only until it must be moved on to a clay pot.

LIVING STONES
(*LITHOPS*)

Lithops is a genus of succulent plants native to southern Africa where rainfall is almost zero. They are commonly called "living stones" because they blend into their surrounding terrain to hide from other living things that are looking for food. These living stones are various shades of cream, gray, and brown, with patterned markings on top. Our gifted fleshy friends have an interesting life cycle. It helps to understand this life cycle so you can respond to their particular needs.

Lithops actually has one fleshy leaf with a split down the center. If you find a *Lithops* that looks like it has multiple leaf bulbs emerging, you have come upon one that is in its shedding and

SUCCULENTS FOR TERRARIUM LIVING

There are certain plant groups that are specifically suited for the small open terrarium. They need bright light or their vivid colors fade. Succulent suggestions for terrariums, vertical planters, or living wreaths are:

Sempervivum (hens and chicks)
Sedum
Echeveria
Graptopetalum
Aeonium
Gasteria
Lithops
Aloe hemmingii (dwarf aloe)
Euphorbia obesa
Crassula (dwarf jade plant)
Haworthia

▲ This simple pebble terrarium highlights two desert wonders of the world, the blue agave and the spotted *Aloe petrophila*.

ABOVE: This Venus flytrap lived in a cleaned sauce jar for several years. It wasn't fed bugs, but the jar was cleaned from time to time. It was not the most perfect living carnivorous plant conditions, but the plant seemed perfectly content in its warm, humid glasshouse.

TOP: Two darling *Lithops* pairs show off their faces to the sun.

growth process. As the seasons progress, living stones will shed their old, outer leaves like a snake shedding its skin. Once those leaves are shed, you will see a new pair pushing up from the center. The outer layer will dry to a point where you can remove it. Then in autumn, living stones will grace us with a small, daisylike flower with soft cream petals growing in a circle (we hope). From such a small creature comes such a great amount of loveliness.

Water *Lithops* during summer and autumn because it can shrivel and die without any moisture at all. But withhold moisture for most of the winter, with maybe just one drink per month.

UNIQUE FOLIAGE PLANTS

Carnivorous Plants

How do you best suit the needs of carnivorous plants such as Venus flytraps and pitcher plants in terrarium designs?

Venus flytraps are the most common carnivorous plant and are a member of the genus *Dionaea*. You might imagine the plant chewing on insects, but flytraps don't chew. The poor insect prisoner is trapped until it begins to disintegrate, and then its nutritious juices are digested by the plant. Here is an absolutely perfect Darwinian example of adapting to survive!

Carnivorous plants often live in bogs. A bog is a sphagnum moss and peat wetland that attracts insects. They fly above the water and plant material, landing here and there. The lovely pitcher plants (*Sarracenia*) have long tubes that rise above the muck. As an insect investigates the inside of the tube, it gets stuck in the hairy lining and cannot fly out. It sounds horrid for the unsuspecting insect, but how very clever of the plant.

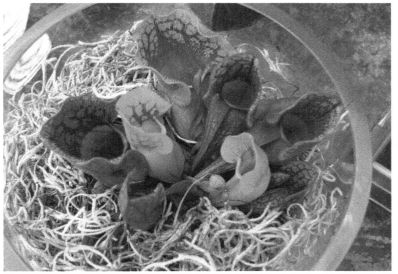

The *Sarracenia* genus is native to the eastern United States, and to bogs in Texas. Many only grow in the swampy terrain of the southeastern United States. You can order pitcher plants by mail. Then you can set up a game for any fungus gnats flying around in your terrarium bog.

Mikado

Mikado, or *Syngonanthus chrysanthus*, is native to Brazil where it lives in boggy soil, indicating a love of peat moss, humus-based soil, and moisture. They are grown indoors or in greenhouses in most parts of the world. Its grassy thatch at soil level provides a base for its upward-shooting spikes, each of which ends with a minuscule, round, cream-colored pompom. It's so interesting, but it's a design challenge too. I suggest planting it in a tall cylinder or vase, or in a conservatory Wardian case.

Baby Tears

Helxine soleirolii, or baby tears, is a standout in a world of wonderful terrarium plants. Green, lush, bushy, and it loves humid

ABOVE: You will find this wonderful pony tail plant in the Beach Life Terrarium in Chapter 4.

TOP RIGHT: A wonderful sweet vine, (*Muhlenbeckia complexa*) that loves moisture. It brings an airy character to any terrarium you plant it in.

TOP LEFT: This is an example of a pitcher plant (*Sarracenia*) in an open glass vessel. I used natural gray Spanish moss to lightly surround the plant and cover the soil.

air. When baby tears are really happy, they sort of stand up and reach for the stars. You can tell when they just love their home. There is no need to mist them in a closed environment; they just drink up the moist air.

Fittonia

Fittonia verschaffeltii 'Nana' is one of my most-loved terrarium plants. It has so much character and strength in design, plus it grows sideways out and low. *Fittonia* plants have bold leaves with striking veins of pink, red, or white that define your design and create visual variety. Their low, sideways growth habit makes them easy to tuck under larger, taller plants or use as a groundcover to cover bare spots of soil. There are many varieties, some with slightly ruffled leaves, and new color combinations are being bred every year.

ABOVE LEFT: The most perfect terrarium plant is *Fittonia argyroneura* 'White Dwarf' because it loves high humidity and indirect light. Remember to trim it occasionally to strengthen its form.

ABOVE RIGHT: *Serissa* are often used as bonsai. They have woody stems, leathery leaves, and clean white blooms. Just think of the formal designs you can create with faux stone benches in glass conservatory gardens with these exquisite little trees. *Serissa* 'Pink Mountain' is dwarf and has pink rose blooms, perfect for a springtime terrarium.

RIGHT: South African squill, on the right, is an incredibly unique plant. *Ledebouria socialis* has a dark green mottled pattern on its long, fleshy leaves that looks like animal fur. The bulb from which it grows is hard and so fabulous. When you plant this specimen in a terrarium, mound up the soil so the bulb sits on top so you can view its structure. Green squill, *L. violacea*, has similar leaf mottling but it is less pronounced and the color seems more true green.

Ledebouria

Both these bulbous wonders of the plant world are fragile. I am always breaking off leaves and swearing in vain. Handle them with care; green squill bends and breaks more than South African squill. I water the squill in the pots on my windowsill well, allow them to drain, and let them dry ever so slightly before the next drink. I suggest planting them in a large, open glass dish that allows the soil moisture to evaporate and which permits proper viewing of the special architectural features of these plants.

Dracaena

Red-edged *Dracaena marginata* is one of those plants that has definite structure. Its spear-shaped leaves grow from the center outward. As you look into this oversized brandy snifter, you see a diverse, stylish display created with this larger *Dracaena marginata* plant. You can drink in the majesty surrounding this kingdom created on sheet moss and black stones. Striking!

Ficus

Ficus pumila, creeping fig, is one of the most fun plants to use in terrariums and an absolute favorite of mine. *Ficus repens* is variegated, with a white rim around the perimeter of its leaves. I love these little vines because of their versatility. They hold up terrifically to humid conditions and grow well. This vine can creep around your terrarium or hold itself somewhat upright.

Oak leaf creeping fig (*Ficus pumila quercifolia*) is my absolute favorite! I love, love, *love* this little gem. It has a wonderful tiny, oak leaf-shaped leaf on a string of a stem, and it loves humidity. Okay, I have fallen hard for this plant.

TOP: 'Janet Craig' has been used in low light conditions for years. Recently, a variety called 'Limelight' is being used that has been breed for its neon green chartreuse shade. If you can find a mini size, use it!

MIDDLE: Commonly referred to as Dragon Tree from Madagascar, the red-edged *Dracaena marginata* is another unlikely terrarium plant choice. So be bold and incorporate a new look!

BOTTOM: This lime green scheme shows off our *Dracaena marginata* above all the rest.

ABOVE: Here is another remarkable variegated creeping fig, *Ficus pumila*.

TOP: The fabulousness of this weeping fig (*Ficus benjamina*) is the white variegation of its leaves. It makes all designs eye-catching!

TOP RIGHT, MIDDLE, FAR RIGHT: You can experiment by growing small specimen plants in clean tomato sauce jars to see how they perform under pressure. A small 2-inch pot with an oak leaf creeping fig in one such jar survived just fine for several years on my kitchen windowsill. Clean the jar about once a year, inside and out, then put the plant back inside. *Ficus pumila quercifolia* plants never waver or brown up—they just grow, grow, grow!

Syngonium podophyllum

Syngonium podophyllum, or arrowhead, is an extremely attractive, strong plant. The young plants form a cluster of upright stems, which makes this a perfect choice for terrariums, especially jungle designs, as they look very tropical. Arrowheads can grow quickly in moist terrarium environments because they are always growing new leaves. If the plant gets too dry, it has a habit of dropping its bottom leaves as they yellow. So make sure the plant receives the adequate water it needs to maintain its strong stems. (You will find a specimen in a triangular glass jar in the Terrarium Design chapter on page 15.

Croton

Codiaeum, or croton, is not your usual terrarium plant. These plants are very tall and big leaved, but that never stopped me from trying to plant them in terrariums. I use them in larger vessels to make bold statements. They don't complain about watering, maintenance, heat—nothing! Right plant, right place is my mantra.

Alternanthera

The variety *Alternanthera* 'Thin Gold' is a fine-leaved, small, wire-like plant. I had never heard of them until I ventured into the land of terrariums and fairy gardens. They like bright sunlight and constant moisture levels, so they are a good choice for terrariums.

Araucaria

Norfolk Island pine (*Araucaria heterophylla*) is a not a true conifer, but it is sometimes called a star pine, triangle tree, or living Christmas tree due to its symmetrical shape as a sapling. As its name Norfolk Island pine implies, the tree is

TOP: Arrowhead (*Syngonium podophyllum*) has large leaf heads and strong upright stems perfect for tropical gardens.

MIDDLE: Crotons (*Codiaeum* species) grow in hot climates such as Florida or the Caribbean, so terrariums suit them well.

BOTTOM: This snow scene contains the pine-like Norfolk Island pine (*Araucaria heterophylla*).

widespread to Norfolk Island, a small island in the Pacific Ocean near Australia, New Zealand, and New Caledonia. It handles humid air and is a nice specimen for forest terrariums, winter snow scenes, or "O Tannebaum" Christmas holiday displays.

Saxifraga

Strawberry begonia (*Saxifraga sarmentosa*) is a darling little, round, fuzzy-leafed plant that has a silvery white leaf pattern on leaves that branch from a center line.

I like strawberry begonias, but mine has given me a bit of trouble (we all have our nemesis). If the leaves become wet, they develop powdery mildew and wither. I started watering it from the bottom of the pot, which gave me better results. Use strawberry begonias in fish bowls and open vessels so there is less chance of water dripping on the leaves.

Strawberry begonia spreads by sending out a long runner that tries to take root and leave the mother plant. You can help them along by directing the runner to the spot where you want it in your terrarium. There's no harm done in cutting them off.

ABOVE: The white polka dot plant is a classic variety. Both the red and white are perfect choices to dress up your designs.

TOP LEFT: Bunched together are strawberry begonia, *Fittonia*, and *Cryptanthus*.

TOP RIGHT: The sweet strawberry begonia (*Saxifraga sarmentosa*) with its soft pads shows off its loveliness.

MIDDLE: Here is the adorable polka dot plant (*Hypoestes phyllostachya*) with red spots.

Hypoestes

Hypoestes is a common plant with thin delicate leaves that do well when the soil is kept moist. It's most often called polka dot plant, and it comes in varieties of red or cream spotted leaves.

TROPICAL PLANTS

Peperomia

Peperomia have so many varieties; some have leaves with bumps, some are smooth, and some are striped. The plants themselves are as strong as an old redwood tree. I exaggerate a bit, but *Peperomia* species are reliable, sustainable, and they can transform a design.

Peperomia puteolata is a great favorite of mine. It is architectural, structural, striated, and strong. It throws up three to four leaves on a short stem spike. In a terrarium, you can surround it with bushy plants, and it will rise above on its pedestal. It leans toward a dramatic effect. This species is easy care, has a good survival rate, and is quite handsome, as all *Peperomia* are.

Peperomia obtusifolia is a charming smooth-leaved plant. I have seen new varieties with pink leaf outlines, called rainbow plant, which make for very pretty terrarium designs. Some have cream, chartreuse, or lime green outlines, or are all green.

Peperomia sandersii is a gem with slivery white brush strokes on its leaf. It's very fine looking!

Peperomia caperata changes direction distinctly, with crinkled leaves that have deeper crevices emerging from a central whorl. These can really play well against other plants, creating variation and interest. It comes in red, too, with a variety named 'Schumi Red'. It seems almost

ABOVE: Parlor palms (*Neanthe bella*) are the bell of the ball and endlessly content in a terrarium.

TOP: Within this Wardian case, you find a tall and stately *Neanthe bella* palm, the yellow spears of a croton pulling our eyes downward, ferns flanking left and right, and our little darlings, the creeping fig, while an arrowhead is tucked underneath on the floor of our tropical jungle. It's quite the proper conservatory collection.

TOP: *Peperomia* are so varied, and these round smooth petals fill any area with pizzazz.

BOTTOM LEFT: Baby rubber plant (*Peperomia obtusifolia*) is the workhorse of the *Peperomia* family: strong, resilient, and enduring!

BOTTOM RIGHT: *Peperomia puteolata* is such an out-of-the-ordinary species and goes fabulously in terrariums.

alien. *Peperomia* 'Meridian', or variegated dwarf *Peperomia*, is similar but the leaf crevices are not as pronounced and its leaves are glossy.

Peperomia rossa has a wonderful two-tone leaf. The rossa refers to the red underleaf. The top of the leaf is a dark green. This is truly a great plant to use for color, leaf structure, and strength standing up to terrarium life.

Pilea

Other terrarium and garden fairy favorites are plants in the genus *Pilea*. It has many permutations of size and color, with tiny creeping leaves on strings of vines

Pilea glauca 'Aquamarine', or blue creeping pilea, is a darling of a plant. It can cascade over mounds of moss or crawl out from under a larger plant. You can couple it with other bluish plants or play it against opposite shades on the color wheel. As a groundcover, it will creep along your terrarium floor and walls. It's terrific!

Pilea microphylla has miniscule green-and-white leaves on soft green stems. This plant is great for very small containers. They are called artillery ferns because they shoot their seeds with a popping sound—sometimes for quite a distance.

The larger *Pilea involucrata* is just amazing. Why it is also called "moon valley plant" is a mystery to me. Try *P. mollis* too; it is a slight variation in all green, with heart-shaped leaves and red veins.

Pilea cadierei, aluminum plant, has a completely different look with silvery, iridescent veins running through the same heart-shaped leaves.

You now have a complete guide to the best plants for your terrarium designs. In the next chapter, I'll explain in detail how I utilized many of the plants described here in completed terrarium designs.

ABOVE: The darling *Pilea glauca* 'Aquamarine' is one of my favorite top plants to use in designs. Its wonderful attributes are its blue-gray color; tiny, round leaves on creeping ground cover vines; and terrific resilient growth. It enhances so many designs.

TOP: *Peperomia caperata* comes in a white variegated form and is a marvelous complement to any design!

MIDDLE: The emerald ripple and the burgundy ripple are the most versatile *Peperomia caperata*.

CHAPTER 6

MODERN INDOOR GARDENING

Japanese-inspired indoor gardening trends are becoming ever more popular. More and more bloggers and magazines, as well as specialty shops, are featuring Kokedama string gardening plants for sale, classes to make your own, and instructions on the steps. I want to inspire you to explore this fun and easy technique. I will share some display ideas for Kokedama creations in this chapter.

Marimo algae balls are also found all over Pinterest pages, in the most otherworldly aquatic scenes. So I *had* to include these fascinating natural wonders in this chapter too.

My profound love of Japanese gardening begins with my deep emotional connection to the Japanese interpretation of nature. I see a natural richness in the moss and stone. I want to share *my* passion with *you*, and I hope it is contagious as you create your own projects.

This *Dicranum* mood moss lives under a diminutive glass cloche on a glass plate fit for royalty.

KEEPING THINGS ZEN

I have had a card bearing an amusing little Zen proverb on my desk for many years. It reads:

when walking just walk,
when sitting just sit,
above all, don't wobble

The moss knew what to do all along.

ALL THINGS MOSS

Moss is amazing. It is soft, green, rootless, and resilient. Run the palm of your hand and fingers over moss and feel its texture. Hold the living moss in your hand and feel its weight when it is wet and soaked with water.

Moss has no true root system and so it can live on many surfaces or substrates. If you walk in a woodland area, you will find moss growing on rocks, bark, in crevices, and on the ground. As a species, mosses are many millions of years old. Mosses have existed since the origins of our Earth.

I have fascinating conversations with people who have discovered this form of plant life and want to know more about it, including, *How do I keep it alive?* The tiny structures of moss absorb dappled sunlight pouring through the tree canopy; they absorb moisture from rain, humidity, and even fog. We have amazing rainforest environments in the northwestern United States and ancient, moss-covered rocks in the deciduous forests of Canada and northeastern United States. Imagining these places gives you a hint of the type of terrarium environment *Dicranum* moss will love.

How Do We Use Moss in Terrarium Designs?

A simple moss sanctuary terrarium is as lovely as home décor. Mood moss in its living form—that is, not dried or preserved—is being sold in small packages that are very convenient for indoor garden projects such as tabletop gardens or traditional terrariums.

The trick to growing moss indoors is to actually give living moss enough water and natural light. Moss will need more light indoors than you might suspect because sunlight streaming into a window is less intense than the dappled sunlight in a forest.

For months, I maintained two large, square trays filled with living mood moss in my home so I would be certain to learn completely what conditions were best for maintaining this new green mass. I would take these moss-filled trays to the kitchen sink and run water over them about every two weeks. Then I drained them and returned the trays to the window area. The moss survived and remained green, fresh, and lovely. A balance between air circulation and moisture is the goal. A larger, lidded, 1-gallon-sized glass container (pictured in the photo) is also spacious enough and has enough air circulation to sustain the moss. A moss terrarium should be kept near a bright, sunlit window. After about five months, I did clean out my container with a bit of dish soap. I ran the moss under water, then drained it on a grate in the sink, and returned the moss to the clean jar.

ABOVE: This living *Dicranum* moss has survived untouched, encased for months, sitting on a bed of black stones, seemingly content.

TOP: You can see the star-like individual sporophytes of a mounded colony of *Dicranum* moss. This exhibits how moss builds upon itself and slowly spreads larger, one sporophyte at a time.

INSIDER TIP:
MOSS GROWING ADVICE
FROM AN EXPERT

David Spain is a moss-growing expert based in Raleigh, North Carolina. He owns Moss and Stone Gardens (www.mossandstonegardens.com).

David, you have been indispensable in helping me to learn about the proper care and uses of moss.

My efforts have always been to get people to appreciate moss as a living plant that we can and should use in our landscapes and also now, to use living moss in containers, including terrariums. I see you as a fellow educator and advocate, spreading the good word about mosses. As long as we strive to better our creations and attempt, as we do with any houseplant, to give it the best conditions we can, it's a good thing. Excellent drainage and sandy, fast-draining soils, like you might use for succulents, are also beneficial.

Are there some practices with moss that you would not suggest?

When people have been exposed to things like the buttermilk/blender method and moss graffiti, which can fail, then that negative experience turns them off to working with moss. They tried what they thought was an easy and unique recipe for working with moss but they end up disappointed.

Why does *Dicranum* moss have different common names? Why is it called mood moss or rock cap moss?

Common names for mosses have been left to regional and haphazard sources. Some names are marketing efforts, like "mood moss" and some were given by regional botanists trying to describe appearance, like "windswept" or "forked" moss. There is no real standard for common names of different species.

However, if a moss is broken into Pleurocarp or Acrocarp, we get a more useful picture of the moss's preferred conditions. All mosses can be classified as one of two types—Acrocarpous and Pleurocarpous. These are scientific categories that describe the growth pattern. Acrocarpous mosses have an upright growth habit, such as *Dicranum* mood moss. Pleurocarpous mosses have a prostrate growth habit, such as *Hypnum* sheet moss.

Dicranum scoparium is a dry shade species that needs to dry out regularly to keep it from forming deposits or molds. This is due to lack of air circulation and natural forces that exist in nature. Moss essentially without natural wear and tear, such as rain, animals, and humans, may not be sustainable in a terrarium forever, but what is? Any basic setup that can allow a container to be fully opened and regularly aerated for recuperation is recommended.

Can living moss survive in a closed container?

It is always a challenge to keep moss in a terrarium, mostly because there's too much moisture and too little air circulation. I prefer working with cloche-topped containers where I can completely remove the cover or with dish gardens that can be taken outside periodically for a bit of Mother Nature. My best advice for moss with any signs of stress in a closed terrarium is water less rather than more, increase the air circulation, or swap out the piece and allow the ailing piece to recuperate outside the terrarium.

Moss that is dormant (dry) will keep for at least thirty days. If you store the moss in a plastic baggy for short period of time, it will be fine as long as the baggy isn't wet or holding condensation inside. If moisture somehow finds its way in the baggy, then open the bag to allow the moss to dry. When you are ready to work with the moss, hydrate the colonies thoroughly.

My guidance to growing exceptional mosses is:

*   *Dicranum montanum*: allow moss to dry regularly
*   *Climacium americanum*: moss good for any type of container, part sun tolerant, bury the running rhizoids at 1-inch depth in planting medium
*   *Leucobryum glaucum*: open-top containers only
*   *Hedwigia ciliata*: moss good for any type of container
*   *Cladonia rangiferina* (lichen): good for open-top container, allow moss to dry frequently, and provide good circulation. Any living lichen can easily introduce fungi in a closed terrarium. Most lichen available on the market has been preserved with glycerin and dyed different, unnatural colors, which are safer to use in a closed system.

I have a small piece of sheet moss (*Hypnum*) that I stuck in a tiny closed spice jar. It has upward strings that you told me are a sign of moss in distress. Can you explain what is happening here?

Your moss is showing leggy growth due to the unnatural conditions, lack of the forces of Mother Nature, and constant condensation. *Hypnum* sheet moss, remember, is a Pleurocarp moss that grows flat. Even if the moss you used was a type of sheet moss, there must have been an Acrocarp mixed in. So, most likely the moss in the spice jar is acting like an Acrocarp, like a *Dicranum*. They are the only ones that grow upward in a spindly spike like that. They can be trimmed and the piece of moss removed to recuperate from the isolation syndrome.

If you see small, brownish-rust spikes with heads growing up from the *Dicranum* moss, then this is the sexual reproduction cycle where the moss produces a sporophyte, which will disperse spores once it is mature. The cycle of life continues in a closed container, as well. ▶

BOTANICAL NOMENCLATURE

Here is a quick lesson on botanical or Latin nomenclature of plant names. It helps when purchasing any living thing and researching plants to know the differences. Which word is the genus and which is the species? What is a common name of a plant, and why is there sometimes more than one common name?

Dicranum scoparium is the botanical name for mood moss. The word *Dicranum* is the genus, and the genus is always capitalized. The second word, *scoparium*, is the species; this name tells us what specific type of *Dicranum* it is. The species name is not capitalized. Genus and species are always in italic.

The common names of *Dicranum scoparium* are mood moss or rock cap moss. If there were a third name in single quote marks after the botanical and species name, that would refer to a breeder's variety (or cultivar name).

Moss is an essential component to many terrarium designs, as well as indoor gardens, miniature gardening, floral arrangements, and bonsai. Return to Chapter 1 and review placement and design ideas using moss with a selection of foliage plants. If the moss inside your terrarium dries out, you can moisten the moss with the streaming mister technique described in Chapter 7, Maintenance, on page 156.

JAPANESE-INSPIRED DESIGNS

Japanese gardens are known for their seasonal beauty. The gardens are an ornamental showcase for plants, ponds, and flowering trees, all existing in abundance. In Japan, a garden means many things: sometimes it only contains gravel and stone. No living things need to be contained in an austere Zen meditation garden. There is also the idea that a garden is a spiritual place, a spot for contemplation and meditation, or to honor a religious temple.

A basic principle in Japanese design is including elements, such as stones, that represent the large-scale landscape, like mountains. The placement of elements becomes important. The Japanese miniaturize the larger landscape, and the terrarium reduces the garden in glass. Both of these ideals parallel each other well in theory and creation.

ABOVE: I walked this mossy path many times at the John P. Humes Japanese Stroll Garden in Locust Valley, on Long Island, New York, to study and interpret its design. Even though it is a small, 4-acre site, I have spent hours there experiencing the incredible serenity contained within its bamboo walls.

INSET: Here you can clearly see the intentional placement of each stone, and you can create this grouping in a terrarium setting. How wonderful would that be?

LEFT: I created a micro-setting on an empty bluestone gravel space with this stone grouping and an autumn fern (*Dryopteris erythrosora*) tucked in the middle as a green focal point that draws your eye to this stark stone grouping. Before I laid the volcanic stones down, I raked the bluestone gravel and handpicked every leaf, twig, and fragment off the area. Your grouping should stand out without competition from litter or other plants. My amateur guess is that this grouping is tall vertical stone with short vertical stone adjacent with reclining stone in front. It has an authentic visual feel and is easy to replicate.

AN INTERPRETIVE PERSPECTIVE
IN STONE AND MOSS

As a terrarium designer who admires Asian aesthetics, I am compelled to infuse my tabletop design with stone and moss. I have chosen a basic stone configuration to incorporate on this interpretive Zen moss and pebble tray, and I have added a moss specimen under a glass cloche.

On the right-hand side of the tray, notice the placement of the tall vertical stone with the short vertical stone adjacent and reclining in front. I also tucked a small pine seedling into the *Dicranum* moss mound. The wet moss will supply the seedling's roots with moisture. I suspect it will live for some time in this setting. This display can be moved indoors with appropriate watering and maintenance, and live easily in a sunny window or on a table.

The air plant loves the open air so I placed it on the bamboo mat, which adds texture. It also connects the separate stone disk and green tray as a visual bridge to move your eye along. This arrangement sits upon a slate tabletop in the afternoon sunlight.

My Zen garden tray layout is uncomplicated yet contemplative. You can take this small Japanese garden concept and create many combinations. I think it makes a lovely backdrop for a tea ceremony with friends. The rock formations are meant to create a pleasant visual effect while not distracting your eye from your peace of mind. Breathe deeply and feel the sun shine on your face .

If I had used natural-colored dry sand or *suna*, instead of gravel or *jari*, then you would have a basically dry landscape or *karesansui*. In my Zen garden tray, sand can replace the pebbles and be raked to create a sand pattern. Then a classic rock configuration can be added. No moss would be needed in that display.

You can bring the photos on page 139 to life in your terrarium. First, lay down a layer of sheet moss in the interior of the terrarium. Small spider plant cuttings would do well to recreate the mondo grass (*Ophiopogon japonicus*) tucked up against the stone lantern and larger upright stone. Add white gravel and flat stones for your path. Maybe you can purchase a small plastic lantern to place upon the moss. I see it coming together already.

Here a sampling of sand designs found in *karesansui* dry landscape gardens. We mimic the world in an ocean of waves or the lines of the earth.

- Straight lines
- Paving stone crisscross
- Flower
- Simple wave
- Whirlpool eddy
- Ocean waves

- Checkerboard
- Curvy lines
- Straight atop with circular curve around a tall vertical stone

STONE INTERPRETATIONS OF JAPANESE-INSPIRED GARDEN DESIGN

These specific stone shapes can be used to represent a mountainous landscape and develop an authentic Asian-inspired miniature garden whether in glass or on a tray.

The shapes of rock in Japanese design can be described as follows:
- Tall vertical
- Low vertical
- Arching
- Reclining
- Flat

Here are several specific stone configurations of Japanese design rock placement:
- Tall vertical and reclining in front
- Tall vertical, short vertical adjacent, and reclining in front
- Short vertical and flat in front
- Tall vertical, flat to left, and reclining to right as a basic triad
- Tall vertical with arching leaning outward to the left, short vertical to right, with flat and reclining in front

Raked sand gardens look simple, so you might imagine that they are easy to create and maintain. In pure Japanese form, the maintenance can take a lot of time, and we must enter into the garden to perform this task. Here lies the lesson that all in life that is *perfectly* beautiful is not without effort.

KESHIKI

There is a modern bonsai master in Japan named Kenji Kobayashi. The inspiration for his work is very close to my ideals of taking the larger landscape and reducing aspects of its beauty in miniature. Whether it's a garden path, a forest, or a streambed, Kobayashi has fused these ideals with bonsai to create an entirely new indoor gardening style called Keshiki bonsai. The word *Keshiki* means landscape.

I have studied Kobayashi's craft in his book *Keshiki Bonsai*. In one example of Keshiki style, moss is utilized in a flat tray with small balls of moss on a flat sheet of moss. Kobayashi suggests it portrays the aerial view of the green islands off the shores of Japan.

Bonsai can take years to master, but Keshiki bonsai can be created quickly with patient hands and small ceramic bowls, repurposed containers, or flat trays. Of course, the elements, plants, and small containers are some of the same basic building supplies used to build terrariums.

In Keshiki bonsai, you use small ceramic bowls with holes in the bottom for drainage. You will want to add a narrow-mesh screen at the bottom of the bowl so the small gravel will not spill out. After adding the screen, fill the bottom of the bowl with a small quantity of gravel, sand, and soil mixed together. Flatten the mixture to create a surface for your living moss to be pressed into. If you add a pine or maple seedling from the garden, make sure it is free of debris and bugs, then bury the plant into the moss. And so your moss bonsai begins.

In a low square traditional bonsai dish, you can plant mondo grass (*Ophiopogon japonicus*), Irish moss (*Sagina subulata*), or Scottish moss (*Chondrus crispus*), any of which would be wonderful Keshiki bonsai plant choices. Use decorative stones to create a narrow valley that snakes through the center.

I cannot wait for you to get started on your first *Keshiki* landscape. When it's completed, set your creation on a bamboo mat, possibly printed with Japanese lettering. Brew some tea and sit awhile, admiring the individual beauty of what you have created.

KOKEDAMA

The word *Kokedama* literally means "moss ball." In *Kokedama*, a plant's rootball is wrapped in sheet moss to retain soil and moisture. The idea has its origins in Japan and is associated with bonsai. In the original practice, soil was formed into a wet ball, and then the plant's roots were planted in the mud ball. Next, the ball of soil and roots were

ABOVE: This is the grandeur of forty years of bonsai mastery. A blue Atlas cedar (*Cedrus atlantica*) is perched atop a moss hill. The trunk has been very skillfully pruned, with specific limbs removed, to create this exact pattern. This bonsai mimics a grove of cedar on a hill but has actually been grown from one plant. It is a glorious example of the miniaturization of our larger natural landscape.

LEFT: This palm-sized world of moss under glass came from the Catskill Mountains of New York State. The style is minimalistic but is representative of the place it came from, the larger forest. The cloche retains a great deal of moisture and warmth. Periodically, mist the mound or remove it to water it in the sink. After it drains, it returns to its home under the dome. It has lasted for over a year.

wrapped in moss, then wired. You can then suspend the moss ball. These hanging creations are called string gardens.

The photo exhibits the beginnings of a cloche design that contains a Staghorn fern wrapped Kokedama-style. Here I have used clear fishing line to wrap the rootball with moss. It is an easy technique. If I were to leave the Kokedama fern under my large cloche, then I would have to mist the moss ball regularly and remove it from the dome for scheduled soaks. It would mostly likely retain moisture longer under the cloche, but not indefinitely. So water maintenance is necessary to keep the plant alive.

I like using staghorn ferns (*Platycerium grande*) because of their wild antler fronds. I had mine hanging by a fishing line in my living room window.

You can set the Kokedama plant in a dish if hanging is not an option. I moved my staghorn fern (*Platycerium grande*) to my kitchen counter and it is pleased with its new site. The kitchen sink is nearby where I can set the plant in a shallow bowl to saturate it with water, allowing it to drink up freely and wet the entire ball. I also mist the fronds lightly on occasion to combat my dry home environment, especially in winter. Keep in mind the heat from cooking on the stove will dry out the plant and moss ball more rapidly, so adjust your maintenance schedule accordingly.

VISITING THE HOME OF MARIMO BALLS

Lake Akan lies in the Hokkaido area of Japan where an ancient people lived thousands of years ago. The Ainu people were indigenous Japanese inhabitants, and their descendants are recognized in modern-day Japanese society. Every October since 1950, when the autumn leaves are vibrant, a three-day Marimo Festival is hosted by local Ainu people at Lake Akan. The festival culminates on the third day with a ritual where an elder Ainu member boards a small wooden boat and returns a few marimo algae balls, one by one, carefully and thankfully, back into the lake. It is a symbolic gesture to remind us to protect the precious balance of natural elements remaining on our Earth and their sacred spirits.

The Marimo Exhibition and Observation Center was built on the shores of Lake Akan in the 1970s and was renovated in the 1990s. The new center is equipped with various facilities to promote the environmental and scientific importance of marimo algae balls as well as conduct research on the protection and propagation of the species.

Research the work of other Kokedama artists. The Dutch artist Fedor van der Valk started experimenting with hanging string gardens in 2011. Websites featuring images of his multi–moss ball, mid-air suspended plants in bloom are lovely and elegant dangling art installations. His fern balls are bold and inspiring works. I find ideas and inspiration from artists like Van der Valk, build on what they have done, and push those ideas forward in my own creations. Empower your Kokedama creative spirit.

Kokedama how-to classes are becoming increasingly available, so check out some of the specialty gardening stores, such as Pistils Nursery (Portland, Oregon) as well as Terrain (Westport, Connecticut) and Sprout Home (Chicago, Illinois, or Brooklyn, New York). I'm sure there are other classes. There is always social media and DIY step-by-step pages on web pages and blogs and, of course, the adult education listings at botanical gardens.

An easy project that can take a few moments to put together is a small water display. This container fits in the palm of a hand, and the marimo ball is just as small. The sweet glass holder, lined with shells and filled with water to the brim, requires only one task every two weeks: You must replace the water with fresh clean water, preferably distilled or rain water (chemical free). Roll the ball in your hand and squeeze out the water to begin the cycle anew.

MARIMO MOSS BALLS

These delightful little balls are actually algae (*Aegagropila linnaei*) and are known as *marimo* in Japan. They originate in Lake Akan, Hokkaido, Japan. The word *marimo* is derived from the Japanese words *mar* meaning "bouncy ball" and *mo* meaning "underwater plant." The gentle currents in the lake keep the marimo green and round as they bounce along at the bottom of the lake. They are also known to inhabit lakes in Iceland, Scotland, Estonia, and possibly Australia. Marimo balls are currently protected in Japan to keep them from going extinct and are considered a national treasure.

How to Take Care of a Marimo Moss Ball

- Marimo moss balls are low maintenance.
- Ensure they are exposed to bright room light.
- Ensure the water temperature is cool.
- Rinse and wash them at least once a week. (You can use tap water, but distilled or rain water is the best for them.)
- Roll or squeeze the algae balls in your hand to keep them round.

FLOATING GARDENS

An indoor water garden terrarium is a fun project, and it's a new and curious use of plants indoors. In their catalogs and on their websites, larger retailers now feature lovely home décor glass vases not filled with flowers but with plants that have their roots visible in the water. The effect is that of raw life, handpicked from nature.

Allowing a plant's roots to float and become part of the design is a new trend that thinks outside the classic pot filled with soil. It also allows us to think of a terrarium in new ways. The definition of "terrarium" has morphed into a loose term that describes any array of plants in glass.

Here, my glass containers look a bit like a laboratory specimen jar holding a science project.

Distinct in their form, the floating water lettuce and marimo balls in this design are unusual by nature. I like this concept, but my aquatic experiment could have included another element, such as a faux coral fan, to fill the space. (Etsy.com is a good place to source plastic replicas, as are pet shops.) Rainwater or distilled water would support the plants' survival; you can also use some activated charcoal to keep the water fresh. I have included marimo balls in this project, but you can keep it simple and float just one plant, such as water hyacinth. You can leave out the stones for a pure, clear display of floating plants.

Water lettuce (*Pistia stratiotes*) is an appropriate name for a floating plant that resembles something you find in your salad. The plant looks great with floating Marimo balls!

WATER GARDEN STEP-BY-STEP ASSEMBLY

1. It was a new experience for me placing floating water lettuce (*Pistia stratiotes*) in water. How do you create a design with plants that move? It was not all that easy. I struggled against the plants until I finally gave in and let them tell me where they should be. I like the view of the hairlike roots below the ribbed green leaves under the water line.

2. Here I am using both hands to hold and place the plant material. When the marimo balls first go into the water, they float to the top. They have not yet had a chance to become saturated. It may take awhile before you can poke them with a stick into their desired placement. On the other hand, the water lettuce floats immediately.

3. The finale outcome is dreamlike and surreal looking. This terrarium may not last forever, but it is *so fun* to watch that its life expectancy does not matter. As you peer down into the jar on the left, the water appears black because the stones are black. I suggest placing your water garden at eye level in a spot where the sun will shine through the water.

There are many water plants you can try and experiment with for unusual displays. With sun rays shimmering through the water, your water garden terrarium can be quite the conversation piece. Plant life in water reveals the spirit of its life force, its roots.

Plant Suggestions for Water Garden Terrariums

- *Pistia stratiotes*   Water lettuce
- *Cyperus papyrus*   Dwarf papyrus
- *Cyperus alternifolius*   Dwarf umbrella palm
- *Caltha palustris*   Marsh marigold
- *Eichhornia crassipes*   Water hyacinth
- *Equisetum hyemale*   Horsetail rush
- *Sagittaria australis*   Arrowhead

Minimal Maintenance

You will have to change the water and maybe get some new plants if the water lettuce cannot hold up indoors. I suggest giving this arrangement as much sun as possible. Water lettuce grows in ponds in full summer sun, so living inside your home will challenge this plant's survival.

Modern Conclusions

Experimentation does not always turn out perfectly, but that is part of the process and—I hope—part of the fun. Explore the different practices emerging from different artists, from various regions and around the world, and start trying them with materials you have available.

Modern indoor gardening crosses over into many aspects of our daily life. We have a desire to decorate the spaces where we spend our time; the desire to be chic, trendy, and up-to-date with the most exciting new styles and ideas; the curiosity to learn new things; and the desire to spend our leisure time relaxing with playful craft activities. All these fundamental cravings can be satisfied with a plant, a jar, and an idea. I wish you many hours of green activities with your new gardening skills!

CHAPTER 7

MAINTENANCE

Is there any plant care at all required for a terrarium? Well, very little, but once you have invested your creative energy planting these fabulous gardens under glass, you'll want them to thrive.

I am one of those people who thinks about plants 24/7. I'm sure everyone does not spend their day obsessed with their plant collection. Well, maybe a few of you do.

When you bring a new plant home, take a moment to discover its basic needs.

- Does it naturally grow in the desert? Rainforest? Marsh?
- Does it go dormant in a certain season?
- Does it like to be wet? Dry? Evenly moist?
- Does it need air circulation?
- Does it love hot, moist, humid conditions?
- Does it thrive in bright indirect light or hot sunlight?

The idea is to establish a small arsenal of care information for each plant. We have filled our containers with healthy living things that we expect will flourish and look great. Here's how to keep them that way.

START WITH BASIC PLANT IDENTIFICATION

If possible, ask the retailer to identify the plants. It helps to know the plant type. What is it? If the retailer cannot identify them, there are many applications that you can download on your phone or computer to help you. Another option is to contact your local Cooperative Extension Service or agricultural office. Many botanical gardens also have plant information services that answer questions from the public. Attaching a digital photo if you send an email can certainly make the identification process go faster. You don't have to be an expert on that species or even know its full botanical name.

Once you have this information, you can then go about building a terrarium that your new plants will love living in for a long time, because you will plan the environment for the plants you have. Plants are just like humans and have certain needs and wants. They'll shout out when they need something, and you'll learn to ask: are my plants thirsty or sick or just fine?

TROUBLESHOOTING

With my background and years of experience, I have an advantage, but I have developed a method that I automatically employ that could be called a visual inventory. It doesn't take very long to develop this practice, and then you will be able to observe what a plant needs in just moments. I simply gather a few detailed clues, just like Sherlock Holmes.

Ask yourself some basic plant care questions:

- Is the soil lighter in color than when it was planted?
- Are any plants leaning sideways?
- Is there a white cottony substance underneath the leaves or in a crevice?
- Are there water drops sitting on your plants or inside the glass walls?
- Are the glass walls covered with water droplets?
- Are there any pesky black flying bugs in your terrarium?
- Are there any yellow, dried, dead, or black leaves that have fallen off the plants?
- Are any plant stems thin and reaching upward toward the sky?

Let's review each situation.

Is the soil lighter in color than when it was planted?

When you plant and build your terrarium, the soil will most likely be moistened and a dark brown color. There is the chance that moisture will evaporate, especially in open-topped terrariums, and when it does, the soil lightens in color, indicating a need for more moisture. The watering section on page 156 will explain how to properly add water to your terrarium without saturating the plants.

Are any plants leaning sideways?

Plants will naturally seek out light, whether it is the actual rays of the sun or bright room lights. When plants grow toward sunlight, there are four possible exposures: eastern, western, northern, southern.

- Eastern sun exposure streams from the rising sun in the morning. It is a strong, warming light, and it moves on quickly.
- Western sun exposure can be very intense, especially in summer months when the days are long and sunlight beats down for hours longer.
- Northern sun exposure has the least amount of sun, and you may only receive brightness in a window facing the north side of your home or building.
- Southern sun exposure can be the optimum option, with strong light bathing a room during most of the midday hours.

Plants receiving light from only one direction will gradually face that direction. You should turn a terrarium occasionally to keep the plants growing properly (evenly) and keep your terrarium attractive. I often turn my terrariums and my houseplants so they have a chance at growing upright. This ensures that all sides of the plants gain the benefits of the light source.

Is there a white cottony substance underneath the leaves or in a crevice?

Mealybugs don't normally appear in terrariums in my experience, but nature will always find a way. Mealybugs appear as a white cottony substance on the undersides or crevices of a plant. Remember in a tightly planted terrarium, you might just want to remove an infected plant altogether to protect the rest of the garden. Mealybugs particularly love jade plants (*Crassula* species) and feed on their succulent leaves. If you see one or a colony, take a cotton swab, dip it into rubbing alcohol, and then dab the little insects to physically remove them. You should be able to keep ahead of them if you perform this practice weekly at first, and then monthly.

Are there water drops sitting on your plants or inside the glass walls?

Moisture is both your terrarium's friend and its enemy. Always be aware of the conditions inside your terrarium and maintain a balance between too much and too little. Mold or fungus is possible with completely sealed terrariums if the condensation level builds up and "rains" down on your garden. Your closed ecosystem has no ventilation hatch or open hole to drain accumulated water out. If water builds up inside, you can wipe the inside of the glass walls or open the lid to give the terrarium a moment to breathe.

Are there any pesky black flying bugs in your terrarium?

These are fungus gnats and they are *pesky*! They seem to materialize out of thin air. They love moisture and feed on rotting debris. Your best defense is keeping your terrarium clear of any dead leaves or rotting stems, and if you need to open the lid or dry out the soil just a bit to reduce their population, then try it. You can always add water back in later. Check with your local garden centers for sticky sticks or traps and place one inside the terrarium to capture the gnats. (Sticky traps or sticks attract the gnats and capture them on an adhesive surface.) Try your best: if the bugs win out, dismantle the terrarium and rebuild it using new soil and clean plants.

Are there any yellow, dried, dead, or black leaves that have fallen off the plants?

Plant leaves react to their conditions by changing color. **Yellow** leaves usually reflect a drying soil. Once a leaf turns yellow, it does not turn green again, so remove it. Check the soil with your fingers. If it's dry, add squirts of water with your mister on the stream setting. Aim the squirts around the inside perimeter glass walls and into the plant rootballs if the soil is very dry. Do not bother with a wide delicate mist because misting does not directly benefit the roots.

Dried or dead leaves indicate that the leaf has dried out and may have fallen off on its own. As the trajectory of the sun moves through the sky in each season, maybe direct sun rays have reached the terrarium and literally baked the leaves dry. Move the terrarium where the sun's rays cannot reach it.

Black leaves, especially if they're soggy, indicate there's too little light with too much moisture, which does not allow the plants to properly create green leaves. Remove black leaves immediately. Check the interior of your terrarium garden, clean up any rotted leaves, remove moss, and rake the soil level with a fork to aerate. You may want to move your terrarium into a more brightly lit area, so photosynthesis can occur properly.

Are any plant stems thin and reaching upward toward the sky?

Sometimes reaching upward is an indication of searching for light that is too far away. The plant may grow leggy, thin, and crooked. Sometimes a plant, such as baby tears (*Helxine soleirolii*) has sunlight reaching it at a certain time of day, which causes the plant to grow quickly and rise up, up, up. You want to control this action because your plants will outgrow their home in a flash. Terrariums survive in rooms where daylight makes the room bright. Put your terrarium on a table, shelf, desk, or counter *away* from a window but in a location that is bathed by light. Terrarium garden plants should not be encouraged to grow rapidly but rather they should simply survive under adequate lighting conditions.

So, now you are an expert terrarium inspector; you will only need to glance at your terrarium to realize it is doing fine without you.

WATERING METHODS

If or when watering is necessary, the procedure is simple.

A simple plastic mister is the most important tool to water your terrariums or most indoor plants and projects. There are two settings on a mister: light mist spray and a high-powered stream. Which one should you use, and when?

Lidded fish bowls create the most condensation that I have observed and will need frequent wiping out with a paper towel. Lidded apothecary jars, cookie jars, or peanut jars usually maintain a stable level of moisture on their own. In six to twelve months, you may want to add a few squirts if you notice the soil

ABOVE: This photo accurately demonstrates the perfect and powerful stream of water that you will be able to direct into the rootballs of your plants with a mister. Air plants prefer a bit more mist with their squirt. When you add additional water, do not broadcast water over the plants, as you would use a hose in the garden, pouring over the tops of the plants. You need to aim the water accurately because you cannot risk ruining your design.

ABOVE RIGHT: Here you see clearly the soft mist option; its spray is wide to moisten moss or soil. I do not suggest misting a closed terrarium because the moisture inside will naturally recycle, causing condensation. An open terrarium may benefit from misting from time to time, especially if the glass vessel is entirely open, such as a dish garden.

RIGHT: In open terrariums, occasionally you will need to squirt water into the rootballs of the plants. You can also give them a misting to refresh the leaves every few months. You might even mist your succulents once a month if you are in a hot climate, or if it's summertime, or if your plants are experiencing dry indoor heat in winter. Remember, plants come from the outside world where (in most areas) it rains, except for in extreme desert climates.

has lightened. I have a peanut jar that has a plastic gasket on the inner rim, which keeps my terrarium perfectly sealed. The mood moss and *Cryptanthus* planted in it have grown in size but they still fit within the inner belly of the glass space. I open it up and peer in occasionally just to marvel at the wonders of nature. But I haven't watered it in four years! I'm smitten.

I recommend one watering alternative for cylinder or square vase terrariums. In vessels that have a long thin shape, you can use a long funnel placed inside the glass vessel, just above the soil line and base of plants (over the roots). Trickle the *slightest amount* of water down the tube of the funnel until it hits its destination. Premeasure about 1 ounce of water in a cup, and pour that down the funnel. After it has soaked into the soil a bit, determine if this is enough. If you see that the water has not sufficiently moistened the soil, just repeat this step. This is an easy way to control the amount of water you apply, and it allows you to hit the spot perfectly.

Becoming a terrarium artist has changed how I care for my own houseplants. It made me think harder about the wild environment where a plant naturally lives. It rains outside, the wind whips the leaves around, the sun scorches them, and the bugs eat them.

So our homes are sterile compared to what plants endure in their natural world. I believe the most important realization for you as a terrarium gardener is that plants outside usually experience rains. The leaves get a bath and drink moisture into their leaf surfaces. So I go around the house misting many of my houseplants during the year so their leaves can absorb some moisture.

I even periodically drag my 5-foot-tall fiddle-leaf fig (*Ficus lyrata*) into the shower for a nice lukewarm downpour. I wrap the pot and soil in a plastic bag so they don't get soaked, then let the lukewarm water pour down. I can almost hear my fig say, "Aaahhh, thank you."

ABOVE: Air plants (*Tillandsia*) benefit from a good soaking. In this photo, only a portion of the plant is submerged. When you actually water your air plant, the entire plant must be under water. Always remember to give them a good shake, and then place them on a paper towel for a few moments to dry.

TOP: Your dry garden terrariums will still need water for the same reasons all plants need water. Squirt around the plant so the water targets the roots. You can mist cactus and succulent terrariums in summer months.

Some fog in a terrarium is okay, but excessive water accumulation can create fungus, rotting, and plant disintegration. So why wait till this happens? Wipe out your glass jar gently so not to disturb or break the plants. In your closed terrariums, the process of condensation will begin again as soon as you replace the lid.

SWEATING AND CONDENSATION

We have learned that terrariums are enclosed ecosystems. Moisture evaporates from the plants and soil, and then condenses on the ceiling or walls of the glass house (terrarium). The water provides warm, moist air for the green landscape to thrive and grow. This mimics our atmospheric conditions, our ocean's waters, and dispersing rain. Without this cycle, we would not continue to exist.

You can ventilate your closed terrariums for an hour or two by propping the lid open on one side to allow some of the deep fog and moisture to escape. Remember, terrarium glass intensifies heat, which in turn can increase condensation.

Lidded fish bowls sweat the most. It seems to be the shape of the bowl that causes the excess. Conversely, fish bowls without lids in a home that is warm and dry will need to be watered with a plastic mister bottle on stream spray at least every two weeks. Here is a quick guide:

Open fish bowls	Water every other week with your spray mister on stream
Closed fish bowls	Wipe out every week and do not water
Apothecary jars	Keep a balanced moisture level; does not need misting
Lidded jars	May need water every three to six months
Cloche	Will need to be wiped out; a single plant will need water once per month
Wardian cases	Most have a window that can be propped open temporarily
Glass globes	Can be misted with a spray bottle on mist, not stream

PRUNING AND REBUILDING

Pruning

Most plants in terrariums grow gradually. Their growth is slowed by the size of their home. You will also be preventing direct sun from reaching your terrarium, which will also slow the growth of the plants. Fertilizing a terrarium is not necessary and should not be done because you do not want to encourage growth at a vigorous pace in a cramped space.

But eventually, pruning may be necessary. If a branch, leaf, or vine grows more than you might consider attractive, then simply snip if off. Plants can grow and encroach on other plants in the terrarium garden or start pressing against the glass. You'll want to minimize both of these actions. Some plants, such as *Fittonia verschaffeltii*, can smother other plants by covering the leaves or parts of a plant and affect the plant's health; they may stop light from reaching the entire garden. If leaves continually lean against the glass walls and they are frequently wet, those leaves may develop fungus and contaminate the interior garden.

You should also prune plants because it helps them to grow strong. You will maintain your design by periodically pruning a vine or plant that grows quicker than the others. Just as our designs' successes are found in the smallest details, so it is with the maintenance of our terrariums. Each task is a small one. We might find that we only need to remove one long-stemmed leaf on an arrowhead (*Syngonium podophyllum*) or the tip of a vine, like that of a creeping fig (*Ficus pumila*) that has shriveled up.

You can use scissors with a long cutting tip, or you can use your fingers and pinch the stem or leaf between your thumb and index finger until your nail cuts through it. In a narrow-necked terrarium, snip off the leaf or branch, allow it to fall, and then reach in with tweezers or tongs to pull out the cut plant material.

For each plant in the photo on page 160, I will note what needs to be corrected and the appropriate maintenance:

- Starting on the left is an arrowhead (*Syngonium podophyllum*), which has roots hanging out of the pot. Before I plant this specimen, I would snip off any trailing roots.

This motley crew of straggly plants should be rehabilitated or sent to the refuse, not planted in your glorious new terrarium.

- The next plant to the right is an *Echeveria* that has not received enough light; the leaves have whitened, and the plant has lost its perfect rosette center. You can put it in a sunny western-exposure window and wait for the plant to green up again, but it may have lost its perfection for your terrarium design.

- The third plant from the left is *Peperomia obtusifolia* with its wonderful smooth leaves and tiered growth pattern. A small offshoot has grown miniature from insufficient light. I recommend pruning that stem off down to the four healthy leaves below it on the next level. Pruning will encourage stronger stem growth.

- The fourth mini plant, *Graptopetalum*, has grown tall and leggy. It does not have a strong rosette structure any longer, and its small succulent leaves do not look healthy. It also exhibits the ability to grow upward and would likely outgrow your terrarium quickly.

- *Pilea glauca* is terrific for terrariums, but if it's left to grow weak without regular pruning, you will find yours looking like this plant. Snip the stems so they can thicken and strengthen even inside your terrarium. Pruning is good for plants.

- In the back row is a ruffle fern (*Nephrolepsis exalta*). These are normally quite bushy, but this one has become thin. I tried to prevent this plant from losing its fronds, browning, and losing its shape, but it did not respond. If these ferns dry out ever so slightly, the fronds brown up. It is not my choice for a fern in a terrarium despite its delicate beauty. If planted, use it temporarily and replace when it continues on a path of frond loss.

- Last, but not least at all, is my nemesis, *Selaginella*, commonly called club moss. This is one of my favorite plants, but it has also been very challenging for me to master its maintenance. I have been successful growing club moss in just the right place with just the right vessel, but not from anything extraordinary that I did. Creating or replicating those requirements is not always an easy task in our indoor spaces.

Rebuilding Terrariums

Rebuilding a terrarium can be compared to renovating your home. You can change one thing or strip the design down to the bare soil and begin all over again.

When a rebuild is necessary, follow this process.

- Remove the topdressing.
- Pull the plants from their spots.
- Clean debris or loose stones off of the topsoil.
- Rake the bare soil level with a fork and tamp down.
- Assemble your basic ingredients.
- Choose new healthy plants.
- Begin planting and building your new design.

First, find a small sauce ladle and *gently* remove all stones, pebbles, or gravel. Remove pieces of moss, bark chips, or any design elements, such as a wooden chair or a plastic frog. Clean out the terrarium down to the bare soil. Assess the soil you have remaining to see if it is free of mold and fungus. If you see the slightest remnants of fungal material, be safe and replace the contaminated soil with new potting mix. Now you have an empty "canvas." Maybe some of the topdressing materials can be repurposed by being placed differently. You can mound up the soil higher on one side of the terrarium to create a hillside.

If you have removed absolutely everything and your glass container is now empty, wash it out with mild dish soap, then rinse and dry completely.

Maybe you only need to replace one dead plant and can reach into the terrarium with a spoon to dig it out. You may find a fork useful to pry the plant up if the roots have taken hold. Always remove any debris left behind, dig the hole a bit deeper or scoop out soil to make room for the new plant.

In your empty canvas, try out some new ideas. You can introduce different topdressing and create a unique landscape that you haven't previously developed. You are the savvy interior designer: create anew.

ACKNOWLEDGMENTS

A heartfelt thank-you goes to my wonderful lifelong friends Arlene and Everett Smethurst, who listen to every detail of my life with fresh insights and illumination. They are forever precious to me. Everett, former architecture editor at John Wiley & Sons Publishers, was instrumental in assisting me get my first publishing job at Wiley. He started me on my way to appreciating the creation of a book.

Thank you to my sister-in-law and forever best friend, Dr. Jan Charlton, PhD, who read every chapter with a red pen in hand. Without her, my life would simply not be complete.

Thank you goes to my *carissima* friend, Rosanna Chiafolo Aponte, fellow Sicilian-American, publishing professional, and author of three books of her own, starting with *Bella Fortuna*. We met at a networking party in New York City and never knew on that night how important we would become to each other.

To Carolyn Stiman: how can you thank someone who takes you from "I can't do this" to "I *am* doing this," and then holds your hand! You have changed my life. That is a very powerful thing to do for someone, and I thank you tremendously.

There are a slew of professionals at The New York Botanical Garden who I must thank because I would never have become a terrarium designer without their support.

Thank you to Richard Pickett, vice president of retail, for creating a space where I could make the magic happen every day. Your endless support has brought me here.

Thank you to Margaret Csala, director of retail, who promotes my every terrarium project and for giving me the time off so I could get these words on paper. Stellar!

Thank you to John Suskewich, book manager, who put his endorsement on the back cover, and promised me the biggest book-signing party ever, complete with mozzarella and prosciutto. Your insights on book writing have been of great value to me.

Thank you to Paula Campbell-Rabe, retail buyer, for ordering every darn crazy piece of merchandise I asked for. Wink, wink! Thank you for the supplies that helped me to create such a great collection of completed work.

Meredith Counts, licensing director, thank you for using my designs on our Shop website and on posters at the Garden that promoted my work as well as the terrarium craft.

Mariane Garceau, our plant buyer, for tracking down just the right plants I requested over and over and over and over again.

Susie Eldridge, for jumping on board and putting me on the Shop Blog front and center!

Thank you to the Shop staff: Lynn Signorile, Connie Crean, and Tiffanie Green for your support and for being great people to work with every day.

And last, but *certainly* not least, Michael Sylvester, associate director of visitors services at NYBG who is my best customer. Michael, you purchase my terrariums for everyone in your family as well as prominent visitors to the Garden, and always have a few on your desk. I so enjoy our friendship. Someday, we are going to open that "Terrarium-Aquarium Shop." Isn't that something to imagine!

Thank you to two very special women who jumped on the publishing workload to help me when I felt buried under the task at hand: Shari Winard, who gave me insights on how to present the vast world of social media to my readers and organized my Twitterverse. Read her blog!

And to Amanda Dornburgh, a budding author herself, who wrote my glossary and resource guide.

To Cool Springs Press and to Billie Brownell, my editor: it was a stroke of luck mailing my book proposal to you. You saw something special in my work and believed in my ability to produce this inspirational modern indoor gardening book. Thank you for picking me to write these words and keeping me on track.

A tremendous thank-you goes to Lori Adams of Hopewell Junction, New York, my photographer who I met at the 2012 Garrison Art Fair. Kismet stepped in again on a June 2014 summer afternoon when I called Lori out of the blue to discuss the book project. She looked at my portfolio and immediately said, "Yes." Lori worked harder than I could ever have imagined she could. She was patient and so eager to create just the right magical photo, taking many shots over again. I love my book cover; you really nailed it perfectly. Thank you, Lori! Check out her website, her books, and her talent! www.loriadams.photoshelter.com.

DEDICATION

To Daniel L. Hyman, my loving husband, for all he does for me every single day that gives me the grace to imagine what can be! And Smudgie, our little rescue kitty cat who is my darling sweetheart girl who agreed to live with us. Daniel, I *absolutely* would never have accomplished this book without you. You lug endless amounts of plants, moss, soil, stones, and glass jars in and out of the car without complaint! You cook the best comfort food that I simply cannot stop eating. Otherwise, I would actually only eat frozen waffles. You and me babe, all the way, till the sun goes supernova.

To Carmela Colletti, my mother, who gets a special citation because at 91 years old, she is resilient! She drives around doing errands for friends younger than she is and jumps on planes to fly across the United States. The greatest lesson that she has taught me is "to persevere." She also proclaimed loudly, "Your terrarium designs look good enough to eat!" That was a very big compliment coming from an Italian! For us, everything reverts back to food. A giant thank-you goes out to my sister, Rosalie Kleeb, who cheers me on through all my crazy adventures in life.

RESOURCE GUIDE

Let this guide be your resource on how and where to find inspiration everywhere!

I want to connect you, the terrarium lover, with amazing artists, designers, vendors, retailers, and the larger terrarium community. You can generate your own artistry, then share it with people everywhere. A terrarium utopia? Maybe, but after all, I am an idealist!

Through social media, we can create our own visual story or watch others bring inspiration to our eyes in seconds. Social media shows us terrariums from around the world, as well as where to find supplies, design ideas, additional education, and connections with others with our same passions.

To get you started, I want to be with you as you evolve into a master terrarium and indoor gardener. My website will give you planting tips, event announcements, and up-to-date trending. My social media pages will provide photos of my new designs, instant access to send me a question, or to post, Tweet, Pin, or Instagram your creations to show what you have created.

Follow my Pinterest boards to lead you to a visual world of beauty.

Maria Colletti Design Studio Contacts

Twitter: @GreenTerrariums
Facebook: Terrariums Gardens Under Glass
Pinterest: Maria Colletti Green Terrariums
Instagram: maria.colletti.399
Website: www.green-terrariums.com

Pinterest followers targeting their craft who "pin" interest in terrariums, air plants, succulents, and mosses are abundant. Find local resources or just browse the followers on my Twitter page till you find your niche. Here is your roadmap city dwellers, suburban dwellers, out in the county, across the pond, and countries abroad such Australia, Jakarta, Brazil! My Twitterverse takes you on a trip around the world. It's a directional guide to the many fascinating tweeters, including websites, who can inspire your future designing, listed in the United States and worldwide. Let's get to it!

UNITED STATES

CALIFORNIA

Plantaflor USA, Inc. @PlantaflorUSA in Orcutt
Sells everything from popular to rare varieties, including the most difficult-to-find air plants.
Website has care tips, beautiful photos, newsletter.
Website: www.plantaflorusa.com
Contact: nancy@plantaflor.com or (866) 458-1010

Oakland Glass Co. @oaklandglassco in Oakland
Handcrafted glass terrariums, planters, and home décor.
Website: www.oaklandglass.com

Urbio @myurbio in Oakland
Vertical gardening and storage: modular, magnetic, and looks great on any wall.
Website: www.myurbio.com
Contact: info@myurbio.com or (510) 899-9724

Gardenista @gardenista in San Francisco
Practical, design-focused gardening with current trends plus links to gardening suppliers.
Website: www.gardenista.com

Succulence @TheSucculence in San Francisco
Plant and lifestyle store that sells supplies of all types and varieties.
Website: www.thesucculence.com
Contact: (415) 282-2212

Juicy Kits @JuicyKits in Los Angeles
Do-it-yourself terrarium kits for succulents and air plants.
Website: www.juicykits.com

Josh Rosen—Airplantman Designs @airplantman in Santa Monica
Website: www.airplantman.com

Oddyssea @Oddyssea_HMB in Half Moon Bay
Shop and garden.
Website: www.oddyssea.com
Contact: info@oddyssea.com or (650) 440-4555

Woolly Pocket @woollypocket in Los Angeles
Vertical planters.
Website: www.woollypocket.com

COLORADO

Chuckle Farm @ChuckleFarm in Denver
Indoor Garden Kits and Garden Musings blog; ideas and inspiration.
Website: www.chucklefarm.com
Contact: hello@chucklefarm.com

FLORIDA

Batson's Foliage Group, Inc. @BatsonsFoliage in Sorrento
Ittie Bittie® Terrariums & Fairy Plants.
Website: www.batsonsonline.com

Russell's Bromeliads in Clermont
Grower and distributer specializing in air plants.
Website: www.russellsairplants.com
Contact: (407) 656-5541

Plantstr @Planstr in Miami
Retailer of exotic air plants that are easy to care for in kits, plus instructions.
Website: www.plantstr.net
Contact: (305) 951-0500

Teacup Terrariums @TeacupTerrarium in Miami
Create little gardens in unlikely vessels, particularly using succulents and air plants.
Website: www.teacupterrariums.com

Air Plant Supply Co. @airplantsupply
"Spreading love one tillandsia (air plant) at a time."
Website: www.airplantsupplyco.com
Contact: info@airplantsupplyco.com or (888) 631-7611

GEORGIA

Southeast Succulents @sesucculents in Decatur
Succulent plants, dish-gardens, handmade hypertufa pottery, vertical gardens and terrariums.
Website: www.southeastsucculents.com
Contact: (404) 314- 8374

Accent Décor @AccentDecor in Norcross
Wholesale importer of high-end home accents, floral containers, and event décor.
Website: www.accentdecor.com

IDAHO

Jerry & Julie Peed @HPotterGardens in Coeur d'Alene
Unique designs in outdoor décor, terrarium, window boxes.
Website: www.hpotter.com
Contact: (509) 921-1640

ILLINOIS

Sprout Home Chicago @Sprout_Home in Chicago
Blog, classes, store, custom terrariums and advice.
Website: www.sprouthome.com
Contact: info@sprouthome.com

KANSAS

Amy Millis @itgterrariums in Eudora
Terrariums by Amy Millis, terrarium kits on Etsy.
Website: www.etsy.com/shop/InsideTheGlass or www.insidetheglass.wix.com/inside-the-glass
Contact: insidetheglass@live.com

MICHIGAN

Shaun J @TerrariumMan in Benton Harbor
Manufacturer of stylish retro and modern planters for home and office.
Website: www.RetroTerrariums.com
Contact: (269) 925-4343, ext. 222

8 Oaks Terrariums @8OaksTerrariums in Grand Rapids
Terrarium maker.
Website: www.8oaksterrariums.tumblr.com
Available for sale at: Blue Door Antiques, 946 Fulton St. E, Grand Rapids, MI 49503

MINNESOTA

Jacie/Moss Love @mosslove in Minneapolis
Blogger and seller of contemporary thematic terrariums and marimo.
Website: www.mossloveterrariums.com
Contact: info@mossloveterrariums.com

NEW YORK

Maria Colletti @GreenTerrariums in New York (Bronx)
Weekly postings of new designs, workshops, and how-to information.

NYBG Shop @ShopintheGarden
The New York Botanical Garden, Shop in the Garden
Website: www.nybgshop.org
Contact: (718) 817-8073

NYBG Adult Education @NYBGAdultEd
Classes on every form of garden, floral, craft pastime.

Nixie Sparrow @NixieSparrow in Beacon
DIY workshop space with beer and wine; including my terrarium workshops
Website: www.nixiesparrow.com
Contact: (845) 202-7011

Sprout Home @sprouthome in Brooklyn
Blog, classes, store, custom terrariums, and advice.
Website: www.sprouthome.com
Contact: info@sprouthome.com

Roots in Rust @RootsinRust in Brooklyn
Organic planters, terrariums, and home accessories for the design-conscious.
Website: www.rootsinrust.com

Jamali Garden @JamaliGarden in New York City (Manhattan)
A unique selection of floral glassware, and indoor gardening supplies in NYC's flower market.
Website: www.jamaligarden.com
Contact: (201) 869-1333 or (201) 869-9143

Luludivingart @luludiframes in Astoria
Blogger and source for interior design products, terrariums and classes.
Website: www.luludi.net
Contact: info@luludi.net or (888) 9LU-LUDI

NEW JERSEY

Kristin Molinaro @EclecticMarimo in Bloomfield
Marimo terrarium designer.
Website: www.eclecticzenmarimo.com

NORTH CAROLINA

Appalachian Tropicals @AppTropicals in Asheville
Family-owned business specializing in stylistically displayed epiphytic plants.
Website: www.appalachiantropicals.com
Contact: info@appalachiantropicals.com or (828) 222-2225

Moss Rocks! @Moss_Rocks in Raleigh
Dedicated to the sale, promotion, cultivation, and creation of unique containers with moss.
Website: www.mossandstone gardens.com
Contact: info@mossandstonegardens.com or (919) 622-4150

OHIO

Anchor Hocking @AnchorHocking in Lancaster
Standard glass container manufacturer and DIY information. Anchor Hocking products are displayed at the Ohio Glass Museum in Lancaster, Ohio.
Website: www.anchorhocking.com
Website: www.ohioglassmuseum.com

PENNSYLVANIA

Moss Acres @mossacres in Honesdale
Moss and accessories reseller, inspiring projects, and connections.
Website: mossacres.com
Contact: info@mossacres.com or (866) GET-MOSS

Sprout Clarity @sproutclarity in Philadelphia
Photos of succulents by Marisa Milerick

ABJ Glassworks (Ashley Bram-Johnson) in Philadelphia
Website: www.abjglassworks.com
Blog: www.abjglassworks.blogspot.com

WASHINGTON

Two Green Thumbs @TwoGreenThumbs
Leader of the trend in miniature gardening.
Website: www.twogreenthumbs.com
Contact: (206) 352-0494

DIG Floral & Garden @DIGNursery in Vashon Island
Retailer of succulents, air plants, terrariums, Staghorn ferns, pitcher plants.
Website: www.dignursery.com
Contact: (206) 463-5096

OUTSIDE THE UNITED STATES

AUSTRALIA

Living Roots @LivingRoots in Brisbane
Terrarium Artist booth at local market
Contact: livingrootscommunity@gmail.com

Gardens In Glass @GardensInGlass in Perth
Beautiful terrariums, made to order.
Website: www.gardensinglass.com
Contact: gardensinglass@outlook.com

BRAZIL

Fabiane Mandarino@terrariosecia in Rio de Janeiro
Terrarium designer.
Facebook: terrariosecia
Instagram: terrariosecia
Contact: info@terrarios.com.br

CANADA

Plant Terrariums @PlantTerrariums in Calgary, AB
Terrariums, quality vintage goods, natural artwork, and indoor gardening.
Website: www.plantterrariums.ca
Contact: (403) 462-6230

Pot Incorporated @Pot_Inc in Vancouver, BC
Succulents, plant containers.
Website: potinc.ca
Contact: 604-862-4273

Brick & Mortar Living @BrickMortarShop in New Westminster, BC
A quaint shop filled with local designs, unique gifts for the home.
Website: www.brickandmortarliving.com
Contact: (604) 553-0289

Minimalistos @Minimalistos in Halifax, Nova Scotia
Handmade terrariums.
Website: www.minimalistos.com

HONG KONG

Puff Terrariums @PuffTerrariums in Hong Kong
Terrarium maker, DIY classes.
Website: www.puffterrariums.com
Contact: info@puffterrariums.com or 852-9743-8887

INDONESIA

Happy Terra @happy_terra in Bandung
Terrarium and cactus crafts maker.
Contact: 082216771155

SINGAPORE, SOUTHEAST ASIA

InOut Atelier
Moss terrarium, figurines.
Website: www.inout.myshopify.com
Facebook: weareinout
Instagram: @weareinout

UNITED KINGDOM

Botanica Home @TBotanica in Glasgow, Scotland
Handmade custom terrariums, plant designs, amazing sand designs for weddings and other events.

Secret Glass Garden @Secret_G_Garden in London
Handcrafted terrariums and DIY kits.
Website: www.secretglassgarden.weebly.com
Contact: via the website

Unique Botanicals @UBotanicals in Whitton, London
Modern natural living art for the home or office.
Website: www.etsy.com/shop/uniquebotanicals
Instagram: @uniquebotanicals

BLOGGERS AND DIY

Design Sponge
www.designsponge.com

Apartment Therapy
www.apartmenttherapy.com

Dirt du jour
www.dirtcouture.com

Stephanie Stuber, Art of Moss
www.theartofmoss.com

Brandi Chalker, CA workshops
www.succulentsandsunshine.com

CRAFT FAIRS

Renegade Craft
www.renegadecraft.com

Indie crafts
www.ice-atlanta.com

Country Living Fair
moswald@stellashows.com

Garrison Art Center
www.garrisonartcenter.org/events_fair.cfm

Hudson River Exchange
www.hudsonriverexchange.com

Indie Craft Parade
www.indiecraftparade.com/blog

Artists and Fleas
www.artistsandfleas.com

Brooklyn Flea
www.brooklynflea.com

RETAILERS

NATIONAL SOURCES

Terrain
Anthropologie
Pottery Barn
West Elm
Crate & Barrel
Target
Wal-Mart
IKEA
Michael's
Jo-Ann Fabric and Craft
Home Goods
Christmas Tree Stores
The Container Store

CALIFORNIA

The Gardener, Berkeley
www.thegardener.com

Flora Grubb, San Francisco
www.floragrubb.com

Roger's Gardens, Corona del Mar
www.rogersgardens.com/rgblog/?p=730

Potted Store, Los Angeles
www.pottedstore.com

CONNECTICUT

Terrain, Westport
www.terrain.com

Ace Begonias
www.acebegonias.com

GEORGIA

Garden, Atlanta
www.gardenatl.com

MASSACHUSETTS

Homegrowntrades
Emily Richardson, owner, 82 Cranberry Hwy Route 6A, Orleans, MA 02653
Shop will feature her succulent collections (appeared in *Better Homes and Gardens*)

MINNESOTA

Honey Shine, Minneapolis
www.honeyshine.net
Features Pill terrariums in February
2015 *Better Homes and Gardens*

MISSOURI

Boxwood Farms, St. Louis
www.bowoodfarms.com

NEW YORK

Ned Kelly & Company, Piermont
www.nedkellyandco.com

TK Home and Garden, Hudson
tessy@tkhomeandgarden.com

Hammertown, Rhinebeck
www.hammertown.com

OREGON

Pistils Nursery, Portland
www.pistilsnursery.com

Artemisia, Portland
www.collagewithnature.com
/welcome

PENNSYLVANIA

City Planter, Philadelphia
info@cityplanter.com

BOTANICAL GARDENS

Check out your area gardens and
museums for workshop listings.

New York Botanical Garden
www.nybg.org

Horticultural Society of NY
www.thehort.org

Brooklyn Botanic Garden
www.bbg.org

Chicago Botanic Gardens
www.chicagobotanic.org

Bartow-Pell Mansion Museum
www.bartowpellmansionmuseum.org

San Francisco Conservatory of
Flowers
www.conservatoryofflowers.org

MAIL-ORDER GALORE

Etsy
www.etsy.com

Amazon
www.amazon.com

Aquarium Plants
www.aquariumplants.com

Aquarium Supplies
www.aquariumplantsandsupplies
.com

Uncommon Goods
www.uncommongoods.com

Black Jungle
www.blackjungleterrariumsupply
.com

Tropiflora
www.tropiflora.com

Glasshouse Works
www.glasshouseworks.com
/terrariumplants.html

Teresa's Plants
www.teresasplants.com
/terriumsupplies.aspx

Violet Barn
www.violetbarn.com/shop

Pet Flytrap
www.petflytrap.com

Hirt's Gardens
www.hirts.com/b/2423837011

Webstaurant
www.webstaurant.com

Home Decorators
www.homedecorators.com

Modern vase and gift
www.modernvaseandgift.com

Pennington Garden
www.penningtongarden.com
/Products

MAGAZINES

Better Homes and Gardens
Coastal Living
Country Gardens
Country Living
Garden Design
Hudson Valley Magazine
Martha Stewart Living
The Cottage Journal
Westchester Homes
Westchester Magazine

The New York Botanical Garden Enid
A. Haupt Conservatory is a very large
terrarium.

ADDITIONAL READING

Beautiful Tabletop Gardens,
by Janice Eaton Kilby

Bring the Outdoors In,
by Shane Powers

Cactus & Succulents,
by Asakawa, Bagnasco, Foreman,
Buchanan

Indoor Garden,
by Diana Yakeley

Keshiki Bonsai,
by Kenji Kobayashi

The Living Wreath,
by Natalie Bernhisel-Robinson

The New Terrarium,
by Tovah Martin

The Plant Recipe Book,
by Baylor Chapman

Succulents Simplified,
by Debra Lee Baldwin

Teeny Tiny Gardening,
by Emma Hardy

Terrarium Craft,
by Amy Bryant Aiello and Kate
Bryant

The Unexpected Houseplant,
by Tovah Martin

The Victorian Fern Craze,
by Sarah Whittingham

GLOSSARY

Acrocarp: A type of true moss with erect stems, with capsules at the tip of the branch. Also called "cushion moss."

Activated charcoal: A solid piece of charcoal that is infused with oxygen in order to increase its adsorptive power. Used in terrariums to absorb impurities.

African violet mix: A soil mix with a bit more on the acidic pH. You can create your own mix with peat moss and vermiculite or perlite using these ratios: one-third potting soil, one-third peat moss, one-third vermiculite or perlite.

Apothecary jar: A tall glass jar with lid. Traditionally used in old-fashioned drug stores (apothecaries) for the display and sale of candies and other bulk goods.

Asymmetrical: Lacking in symmetry.

Binomial: Using or having two names; applied to the system of naming plants introduced by Linnaeus, in which every plant receives two names, one indicating the genus, the other the species; for example, *Bellis perennis*, the English daisy.

Bog: A mire that accumulates peat, a deposit of dead plant material—often mosses, and in a majority of cases, sphagnum moss. It is one of the four main types of wetlands.

Cactus mix: Potting mix for cactus and succulents that contains sand.

Carnivorous plant: A plant found in bogs that traps and "digests" small insects in order to gain the nitrogen usually lacking in the wet soils where it lives; includes plants such as Venus flytrap or pitcher plants.

Cloche: A bell-shaped cover used to protect a plant from frost or cold; an individual cold frame.

Compote dish: A glass, porcelain, or metal bowl that has a base and stem, traditionally used for serving compotes, fruits, and nuts.

Condensation: The act or process of reducing a gas or vapor to a liquid or solid form.

Debris: Loose fragments of material such as soil, broken rock, or plant material.

Drainage: A means of removing excess water or moisture.

Epiphyte: In botany, a plant that grows on another plant but which does not derive its nourishment from it: includes plants such as many ferns, orchids, and bromeliads.

Equilibrium: The condition that exists when a chemical reaction and its reverse reaction proceed at equal rates, creating balance for an environment. An example is when a terrarium reaches a balance between moisture and air circulation.

Fertilizer: Material added to soil or the plant itself to provide additional nutrients.

Fish bowl: A glass vessel, usually with two mostly flat faces, ½- to 1-gallon capacity. Traditionally used for housing one or two goldfish or other tropical fish.

Footed bowl: A round glass bowl with an extended glass foot at bottom for added stability and style.

Forcing spring bulbs: Causing bulbs to grow indoors out of season.

Found object: Something found in the outdoors, in our natural surroundings.

Frond: A leaf of a palm or fern.

Fungus: Any of a diverse group of eukaryotic single-celled or multinucleate organisms that live by decomposing and absorbing the organic material in which they grow, including mushrooms, molds, mildews, smuts, rusts, and yeasts, and classified in the kingdom Fungi or, in some classification systems, in the division Fungi (*Thallophyta*) of the kingdom Plantae.

Genus: The usual major subdivision of a family or subfamily in the classification of organisms, usually consisting of more than one species.

Hurricane glass: A glass cylindrical shape with a wider center section. Can be used to enclose candles to keep the wind from blowing around the flame.

Lantern: Portable glass-sided lighting device.

Marimo: Balls of algae originating in Lake Akan, Hokkaido, Japan.

Moss: A common name for low-growing, nonflowering, rootless plants that lack a vascular (circulatory) system, of the class Musci. Other genera are called mosses, such as *Lycopodium* (club moss) and *Selaginella* (little club moss or spike moss), but these are not true mosses since they have vascular systems.

Nomenclature: For the purposes of this book, the international vocabulary of Latin names for kinds of plants, standardized by commissions set up by the appropriate taxonomic experts.

Petal: One of the often colored segments of the corolla of a flower.

Photosynthesis: The chemical reaction, powered by energy from light, by which carbon dioxide from the atmosphere combines with water to produce oxygen and the sugars that the plant uses to provide energy for its growth, reproduction, and tissue repair. Photosynthesis mainly takes place within the leaves and is normally mediated by light-sensitive pigments known as chlorophylls.

Pigmentation: The natural coloring of plant tissue.

Pleurocarp: A type of true moss with creeping stems that tends to grow in interwoven mats. Also called "carpet moss."

Potbound: Having roots so densely grown as to fill the container and require repotting.

Potting mix: A mix of sterilized soil, perlite, and vermiculite. The perlite and vermiculite add bulk without much weight. Some brands also include fertilizer in the mix.

Rootball: Where the roots of a plant grow in the soil creating a tight-knit maze of roots.

Seedling: A plant or tree grown from seed.

Species: The major subdivision of a genus, regarded as the basic category of biological classification, one that is not a hybrid or variety. Knowing the species of a plant assists in the identification of chosen plant.

Sphere: A geometrically perfectly round, circular object.

Sporophyte: The form of a plant, particularly moss, that produces asexual spores.

String garden: A suspended Japanese garden made by inserting a plant's rootball into a wet soil ball, and then wrapping the soil ball it with moss and wire.

Substrate: The medium on which an organism lives, such as soil or rock.

Succulent: A plant that has thick, heavy leaves used to store water.

Temperate zone: The part of the Earth's surface lying between the Tropic of Cancer and the Arctic Circle in the Northern Hemisphere or between the Tropic of Capricorn and the Antarctic Circle in the Southern Hemisphere, and characterized by having a climate that is warm in the summer, cold in the winter, and moderate in the spring and fall.

Topdressing: Gravel, river stones, or glass chips put on top of the soil as decoration but also which also assist in retaining moisture.

Variety (plant): The name (usually shown in single quotes) that provides its breeder with some legal protection for the name of cultivated plant (a cultivar) as a special variety.

Variegation: The conjunction of two or more colors (such as white and green) in the petals, leaves, or other parts of plants.

Vessel: A jar or glass container with a plain or fancy shape, into which a terrarium can be built.

Wardian: An early type of sealed protective container for plants. An early version of the terrarium, invented by Dr. Nathaniel Bagshaw Ward (1791–1868).

INDEX

MEET MARIA COLLETTI

Maria Colletti earned degrees in Horticulture and Cultural Antropology before starting her career working for a terrace gardening firm in New York, planting outdoor gardens. Colletti furthered her career with an interior plantscaping firm, working at sites maintaining the office buildings for corporations such as IBM and Xerox. At the time, Xerox won awards for its large and spectacular lobby entrance with its high ceiling and skylights. Not to be outdone, IBM built enormous atriums with bamboo trees, hanging vines, and gurgling fountains. The firm promoted Maria to Manhattan midtown manager, where she managed a dozen or so plant technicians. Maria had her own accounts maintaining the plants in many large atriums including the Guggenheim Museum and the executive offices and studios of ABC Television. Maria has since been the store manager of the Shop in the Garden at The New York Botanical Garden, Bronx, New York, where her career designing terrariums began.

Colletti has taught classes since 2010 and can be found on the roster of continuing education programs for Westchester Community College as well as The New York Botanical Garden, Bartow-Pell Mansion Museum, Bronx, and Nixie Sparrow of Beacon, New York. Colletti has experimented with desert scenes, tropical gardens, orchids, Irish moss—anything that might live in a glass jar, especially *Selaginella* and *Dicranum* mosses. In *Terrariums: Gardens Under Glass*, her first book, she shares all that she has learned over the years so *you* can enjoy modern indoor gardening too. For her, it is all about the journey, learning everything along the way, and sharing her terrarium knowledge with *everyone*. See page 165 for a list of ways to stay in touch with Maria via social media.

9 781591 866336